is examined. For such a study, George MacDonald
provides an ideal subject, for he is possibly
unique in having achieved distinction in both
fictional types.

R

GEORGE MacDONALD

by Richard H. Reis

George MacDonald is beginning to be rediscovered
as one of the major literary figures of the nineteenth century, and this book attempts to assist
in that rediscovery. For although most readers still
are unfamiliar with MacDonald's works or even
his name, his importance and genius have recently
been recognized by such distinguished critics as
C. S. Lewis and W. H. Auden, his works are
being reissued with increasing frequency after
having been long out-of-print, and he is beginning
to be read again.

Among other things, this volume examines the
reasons why MacDonald was widely known in his
own time, forgotten for the first half of the
twentieth century, and "rediscovered" of late. It
is a curious story. For in his own day MacDonald
was an immensely popular writer of conventional
novels possessing what we now think of as the
worst faults of Victorianism—sentimentality, verbosity, and melodramatic formulaism: boy-meets-
and-marries-girl-after-foiling-villain, young-man-
grows-up-and-finds-God-and-therefore-himself, and
so forth. Such ephemeral fiction *deserves* to be
forgotten, and has been, except by the dustiest
of scholars. Yet in between his novels, MacDonald
produced half-a-dozen strange symbolic fantasies
which were ignored by his contemporaries, and
which have begun to be appreciated as masterpieces only recently. It is a study in shifting and,
we may hope, improving tastes; this work not only
examines MacDonald's best (and worst) writing,
but also analyzes a phenomenon of literary history.

Prof. Reis's study of MacDonald also has another
and still broader purpose. Because MacDonald's
fiction, both "realistic" and symbolic, was consciously didactic, and because symbolic fiction is
not yet very widely understood, the very nature
of conventional and unconventional literary genres

ssociate Professor of English
ssachusetts University, and
Massachusetts, on Buzzards
Cape Cod. He was born in
etts, in 1930, and grew up
od, New Jersey. He began
niversity in 1955, and has
n ever since, at Brown, at
(Chestertown, Maryland),
hool since 1965. Dr. Reis
ummer sessions at Brandeis
University of Kentucky.

academic work, Professor
cal writer and has worked
cy, but his primary interests
iterature. He is the author
holarly articles, as well as
es. His interest in George
Brown in 1955, at the sug-
. Foster Damon. Besides
e has engaged in scholarly
natorial mathematics, and
rest arising from the fact
nteenth-century house and
the 1600's. He prefers to
even as a teacher and
courses in the English
vel, Victorian literature,
poetry, Romanticism, and

d from Phillips Academy
ts, and holds degrees from
 (A.B. in English) and
. and Ph.D. in English).

From Greville MacDonald,
George MacDonald and his Wife
(New York: Dial Press, 1924).
Photo by Lewis Carroll

GEORGE MacDONALD

George MacDonald

By RICHARD H. REIS

Southeastern Massachusetts University

Twayne Publishers, Inc. :: New York

"O heavens! die two months ago, and not forgotten yet? Then there's hope a great man's memory may outlive his life half a year; but, by'r lady, 'a must build churches then . . ."

—Shakespeare
Hamlet, III, ii

In memory of
S. Foster Damon and Charles Philbrick
who can never be forgotten

Preface

This critical-analytical study attempts to provide a useful addition to the recent revival of interest in George MacDonald, whose literary reputation was in eclipse between his death in 1905 and about 1950. The recent publication of books about MacDonald and reissuing of his best work, which had been out of print for decades, may be indicative of another "revival" of interest in a literary figure once forgotten, then gradually rediscovered and restored to importance. Such phenomena are of great interest in literary history, indicating as they do shifts in taste and appreciation of considerable significance.

The chief problem inherent in an examination of MacDonald's accomplishment is that, while he wrote poems, conventional novels (for which he was most famous in his lifetime), criticism, and in nearly every other imaginable genre, his claim to a permanent place in English literature must probably rest upon his few fantastic, visionary, or symbolic works, for both children and adults. Of paramount interest, from the point of view of literary history, is the fact that such symbolic literature was decidedly "out of style" in the Victorian period when MacDonald wrote. The period was the golden age of the realistic novel and the prose essay, but not of symbolic fiction; MacDonald was one of the few writers of his time who practiced the latter art, which has in the twentieth century become far more important than it was in the nineteenth. Only fairy tales, of which MacDonald is a master, had much importance in Victorian England as symbolic literature.

The adult world wanted novels, so MacDonald wrote them because he had to make his living as a writer. Yet George Mac-Donald's literary profession was in a sense only a secondary calling; primarily, he thought of himself as a preacher, a moralist, even a divine. Denied an "official" pulpit because of his unorthodoxy, MacDonald chose to give his message to the world in fiction which was consciously didactic. The result was a series of rather bad (though very popular) novels and a few interspersed master-pieces of symbolic literature, a genre to which didacticism is per-fectly suited.

An understanding of MacDonald's place in literature involves, therefore, all of the aspects of his career which I have examined in the pages which follow: his life, the central philosophical ideas behind his "teachings," his attempts to teach through the popular and best-selling genre of his time, his occasional and immortal ventures into the unpopular symbolism for which he will be remembered, the nature of symbolism in general and its effects upon MacDonald's works, and the influence of conscious didacticism upon the works of those literary figures who prac-tice it.

I have begun by relating the important events in MacDonald's life, with especial emphasis upon those circumstances which im-pelled him toward a literary career and toward the particular *kind* of literature which he produced. From the viewpoint of his work, no doubt the most important event in MacDonald's biography was his being denied a pulpit after having felt a vocation to the minis-try; he felt that he had to find another medium through which to disseminate his essentially religious message, and he chose litera-ture as that medium.

In Chapter 2, therefore, I shall examine the rather unsystema-tized system of ideas which MacDonald desired to embody in his works. For, in a sense, what he wanted to say is as important for a full understanding of his work as the means he found to say it. Although this examination of MacDonald's ideas is moti-vated by, and subordinated to, a desire to understand his art, those ideas are also of some interest in themselves. Rarely original and usually traceable to earlier writers, MacDonald's ideas are nevertheless synthesized in an original fashion. He managed to fit together concepts from such apparently disparate areas as religion, psychology, social and political criticism, and literary theory into an interlocking vision. Yet I must state that, to some extent, I may have imposed a certain artificial order and system upon materials which MacDonald himself never formally summed up into a consciously articulated "system." The wholeness and unity of his vision was so taken for granted by its possessor that he felt no need to declare it. I do not believe that I have done violence to that order by pointing it out as its author never really did.

Chapters 3 and 4 of this study examine in turn the works of conventional nineteenth-century realism and those of the sort which may be variously called imaginative, symbolic, fantastic, or visionary. This portion of my volume explores not only the works themselves, but also the nature of the distinction between the two kinds of writing—a distinction which is sometimes blurred by hybrid forms such as *At the Back of the North Wind* and *The Portent*. But because the realistic works are so many, I have not covered each of them at length. Instead, I have examined in some detail what I consider MacDonald's best conventional novel, *Alec Forbes of Howglen,* and for the rest imagined a "typical" work, displaying the salient attributes of the whole corpus. Such a procedure has not been necessary in the chapter on the imaginative fiction, since there is much less of it; I have here dealt in some detail with all of MacDonald's significant symbolic works.

In Chapters 5 and 6, I have tried to reach some general conclusions about the nature of symbolic and didactic literature, both as reflected in George MacDonald's works and from the broader perspective of literary history and theory as a whole. For it is my contention that MacDonald's significance perhaps exceeds his excellence—that he is important more for what he shows us about the nature of literary genres and of the changes of taste with time than for the independent quality of his work. This is not to say that *all* of MacDonald's works are minor, although most of them are. He did produce a few masterpieces of symbolic fiction which are in my opinion permanent, even immortal, despite and transcending the limitations of his time. Indeed, in my concluding chapter, I point out some of the attributes of the Victorian period which MacDonald so interestingly exemplifies in both its excellences and its defects.

The original stimulus of this study came from the late Professor S. Foster Damon of Brown University, who first called my attention to MacDonald in 1955. I am equally indebted to Brown University's late Professor Charles H. Philbrick, who helped me for many years as both mentor and warm personal friend. Because both of these admirable men died during the final year of this work's preparation and because both would have liked to see it published, I can now thank them in no other way than to dedicate this effort to their memories.

I must also acknowledge the assistance of Professors George K. Anderson, Leicester Bradner, Hyatt H. Waggoner, I. J. Kapstein, and Edward A. Bloom of Brown University; all helped in this study, though none of its defects are theirs. My wife Kathleen has helped enormously, and so has Professor Sylvia Bowman, whose editorial advice has been of immense value to me.

RICHARD H. REIS

Marion, Massachusetts

Contents

Preface

Chronology

1. Not Forgotten Yet   17
2. MacDonald's Ideas   31
3. The Realistic Fiction   52
4. The Imaginative Fiction   75
5. The Symbolic Muse   106
6. The Didactic Muse   125
7. Some Conclusions   138

    Notes and References   145

    Selected Bibliography   153

    Index   157

Chronology

1824 December 10, George MacDonald born in Huntly, Aberdeenshire, Scotland.

1840 Entered the University of Aberdeen.

1842 Dropped out of the university for a year to earn some money cataloguing the library of an unidentified private mansion in the north of Scotland. Presumably fell in love with, but was rejected by, the daughter of the household.

1843 Returned to the university, his original interest in chemistry now augmented by a fascination with German Romantic literature, presumably encountered at the library.

1845 Received a master's degree in chemistry and physics at Aberdeen.

1845– Wandered to London as a tutor, undecided about his life's
1848 work. Eventually decided to become a Congregationalist minister. During this time he met his future wife, Louisa Powell.

1848 Entered Highbury College, London, a Congregationalist divinity school.

1850 Graduated with a divinity degree.

1851 Assumed his first and last pastorate at the Congregationalist Church of Arundel, near London; married Louisa Powell; published his first work, a translation.

1853 Dismissed by his congregation, evidently for heterodoxy; resolved to spread his "message" through making writing his second career.

1855 Published the long poem *Within and Without*.

1858 Published the prose fantasy *Phantastes* and his first book of *Poems*. Received financial support from Lady Byron, the poet's widow.

1863 The first realistic novel, *David Elginbrod*.

1864 *Adela Cathcart,* a novel containing brief interpolated fantasies; *The Portent*.

1865 *Alec Forbes of Howglen,* MacDonald's best novel.

1867 *Annals of a Quiet Neighborhood; Dealings with the Fairies* (later reissued as *Cross Purposes*); *The Disciple and Other Poems; Unspoken Sermons, First Series.*

1868 *Guild Court, Robert Falconer, The Seaboard Parish.*

1870 *The Miracles of Our Lord* (sermons).

1871 *At the Back of the North Wind, Ranald Bannerman's Boyhood, Works of Fancy and Imagination.*

1872 *The Princess and the Goblin, The Vicar's Daughter, Wilfrid Cumbermede.* About this time MacDonald was quite close to John Ruskin and made a profitable lecture tour of the United States.

1873 *Gutta Percha Willie: The Working Genius.*

1874 *England's Antiphon* (MacDonald edited this anthology of religious poetry).

1875 *Malcolm.*

1876 *Thomas Wingfold, Curate; St. George and St. Michael; Exotics* (translations from German poetry).

1877 *The Marquis of Lossie.* MacDonald received a civil list pension of 100 pounds yearly from Queen Victoria. Acquired a residence in Bordighera, Italy, where he spent his winters thereafter. By now he was an eminent Victorian.

1879 *Sir Gibbie; Paul Faber, Surgeon.*

1880 *A Book of Strife, in the Form of the Diary of an Old Soul* (poems).

1881 *Mary Marston.*

1882 *Castle Warlock* (also published under the title of *Warlock O'Glenwarlock*), *Weighed and Wanting, The Gifts of the Christ Child and Other Tales* (later reissued as *Stephen Archer and Other Tales*), *Orts* (later reissued as *A Dish of Orts* and, with a minor deletion, as *The Imagination and Other Essays*).

1883 *Donal Grant, A Threefold Cord* (poems by MacDonald and two others), *The Princess and Curdie.*

1885 *The Tragedie of Hamlet* (a critical edition of Shakespeare's First Folio text); *Unspoken Sermons, Second Series.*

1886 *What's Mine's Mine.*

1887 *Home Again.*

1888 *The Elect Lady.*

1889 *Unspoken Sermons, Third Series.*

Chronology

1890 *A Rough Shaking.*
1891 *There and Back, The Flight of the Shadow, A Cabinet of Gems* (an anthology of English Renaissance poets edited by MacDonald).
1892 *The Hope of the Gospel* (sermons).
1893 *Heather and Snow.*
1895 *Lilith.*
1897 *Rampolli* (translations), *Salted with Fire.*
1905 George MacDonald died at the age of eighty.

CHAPTER 1

Not Forgotten Yet?

I *The Bubble Reputation*

UPON opening Amy Cruse's *The Victorians and Their Reading* (1935), one sees a curious frontispiece: a composite photograph that pictures a group of eminent Victorian writers against an apparently sketched-in background of bookshelves. The men in the picture are J. A. Froude, Wilkie Collins, Anthony Trollope, W. M. Thackeray, T. B. Macaulay, E. G. Bulwer-Lytton, Thomas Carlyle, Charles Dickens—and George MacDonald. One can imagine a modern student of the period asking himself "Who is George MacDonald, and what is *he* doing here?"

Such a question would not have occurred to most of MacDonald's contemporaries. Instead, they might have expressed surprise to learn that he would be largely forgotten by the middle of the twentieth century; for, throughout the final third of the nineteenth century, George MacDonald's works were best sellers, and his status as a sage was secure. His novels sold, both in Great Britain and in the United States, by the hundreds of thousands of copies; his lectures were popular and widely attended; his poetry earned him at least passing consideration for the laureateship; and his reputation as a Christian teacher was vast. This exalted one-time popularity alone makes MacDonald a figure of some significance in literary history; for, it should be emphasized, his was not merely the vulgar vogue of the ordinary popular writer who is successful in the marketplace but is never taken seriously by qualified critics and is forgotten with justice and mercy. In a certain sense, MacDonald may be called a time-server, one who catered to a debased popular market; but he cannot be dismissed as a mere lightweight. In his own time, MacDonald was esteemed by an impressive roster of English and American literary and religious leaders. He was among the closest friends of John Ruskin and Charles Dodgson; and he moved as a peer in the company of

Alfred Tennyson, Charles Kingsley, F. D. Maurice, R. W. Gilder, Harriet Beecher Stowe, Oliver Wendell Holmes, Samuel Clemens, and H. W. Longfellow. All of them respected, praised, and encouraged him, yet his reputation has nearly vanished while theirs survives. One wonders why—and I shall try to explain the phenomenon.

I do not mean to suggest that MacDonald has been entirely ignored in the twentieth century. Indeed, although he is little known among the general reading public, MacDonald has received considerable scholarly and critical attention during the past twenty years. G. K. Chesterton was among the earliest twentieth-century critics who found MacDonald's "message" of importance to the post-Victorian sensibility. Chesterton once referred to MacDonald as "one of the three or four greatest men of the nineteenth century." [1] And when the novelist's eldest son, Greville MacDonald, wrote the monumental biography *George MacDonald and His Wife* (1924), to commemorate the centennial of his father's birth, G. K. Chesterton wrote a laudatory critical essay to serve as the volume's introduction. Like more recent critics, Chesterton found the symbolic fairy tales and fantasies for both children and adults better than the conventional novels which had made MacDonald famous in his lifetime. Primarily, however, Chesterton seems to have valued MacDonald as a religious teacher whose ideas were powerfully symbolized rather than directly stated in the best of his works.

It seems curious that MacDonald's characteristic twentieth-century appeal should be felt more strongly by orthodox Christians, for he himself was a passionate dissenter. Yet probably the most significant volume in the sparse modern MacDonald bibliography is *The Visionary Novels of George MacDonald*,[2] a reissue in one volume of *Phantastes* and *Lilith,* edited by Anne Fremantle, the noted Roman Catholic essayist, and with an introduction by W. H. Auden, who is an Anglican vestryman. Auden's introduction is a valuable critical appreciation to which I shall refer repeatedly.

But perhaps the most important of MacDonald's modern critics is the late C. S. Lewis, still another advocate of Christian orthodoxy. Lewis has repeatedly acknowledged MacDonald as his "master," as the man whose works inspired Lewis's own fantasies and Christian theological writings. In his autobiographical *Sur-*

prised by Joy (1955, 169–71), Lewis describes how reading *Phantastes* began his self-conversion from a cool skeptic to a warm Christian. And in a Dantean treatment of a voyage to the underworld entitled *The Great Divorce* (1946), Lewis makes MacDonald his Virgil, his guide and mentor. Another Lewis volume, *George MacDonald: An Anthology,*[3] is a formal acknowledgment of the debt, consisting of a selection of passages from MacDonald's works. Although the excerpts are mostly from the sermons, and of philosophical rather than literary interest, Lewis introduced them with a brilliant preface which until recently was the most important modern criticism of MacDonald's works.

As an author of fairy tales, which are unfortunately not often taken seriously as literature, MacDonald has largely maintained a reputation undimmed by the shifts in taste which have obscured his popularity as a novelist. The fairy tales continue to sell and to be reissued; in fact, editions of *The Princess and the Goblin* and *The Princess and Curdie* have been published within the past few years, under the sponsorship of Auden and Lewis. Even the novels, ignored by most literary historians nowadays, are still read, especially in Scotland, where the dialect works have always been popular.

Finally, another sign of revived interest in MacDonald's works is the publication of a full-length study by Robert Lee Wolff entitled *The Golden Key: A Study of the Fiction of George MacDonald.*[4] Professor Wolff's book is uneven and at times unsound, but its appearance provides additional evidence that MacDonald is not forgotten yet. Unfortunately, Wolff's volume, largely biographical and psychoanalytical in its orientation, is of little critical value. Wolff's insistence upon treating literature as a half-inadvertent revelation of an author's psychic troubles is interesting doctrinaire Freudianism that should not be mistaken for literary criticism. It is to be hoped, however, that the appearance of this rather sensational study will stimulate the slow current revival of interest in George MacDonald.

II *MacDonald's Life*

Although Greville MacDonald's exhaustive biography of his father has relieved me of any obligation to chronicle MacDonald's life at length, it does seem appropriate to review the facts of his career briefly. The son's biography is, naturally, the source of most of these facts; and it is sufficiently authoritative not to require correction. *George MacDonald and His Wife* is invaluable as a source of information, as a repository of letters unpublished elsewhere, and, to a lesser extent, for its earnest but rather inexpert critical commentary. I must stress, however, that the biography displays the faults of many such works by the sons of notable fathers. Greville MacDonald insists that his father was the best writer and wisest man who has ever lived and that he has been maligned and misunderstood by the ignoramuses who fail to concede the point. It is very likely, indeed, that there may have been some glossing over of useful facts in the son's anxiety to portray the father in the best possible light. This filial piety seems to have inspired Robert Lee Wolff's speculative efforts to throw some light upon the darker places in MacDonald's psyche.

Details of MacDonald's early life are of greatest significance for a critical understanding of his works. Many of his novels, especially, are in part autobiographical; and, as is often the case with autobiographical writers, the novels focus on his upbringing and on his earliest encounters with the world of practical affairs. Therefore, we need to know that MacDonald was born in Huntly, Aberdeenshire, in 1824, and that he grew up there and in nearby Pirriesmill, where his father established a somewhat larger farm not long after George was born. His boyhood was set in a traditional rural atmosphere, compounded of Calvinist hellfire, oatcakes, horsemanship, agricultural virtues, and exploration of neighborhood ruins and wildernesses. Reminiscences of such adventures, portrayed with vigor and immediacy, occur again and again in MacDonald's most convincing realistic novels, constituting a large part of his charm as they do of Dickens's. It should not be supposed, though, that MacDonald's own family was conventionally Calvinistic: his father was a nonsectarian Christian of the sort which values the Bible more than what anybody says about it. Nevertheless, the prevailing sternness of Presbyterian Scotland was always there, an oppressive, ubiquitous force.

Greville MacDonald maintains that George's father was infinitely noble and that his relations with his son were exemplary. C. S. Lewis adds that this rare rapport between father and son must account for MacDonald's ideal of the transcendent Fatherhood of God. George, if we are to believe Greville, never asked his father for anything without getting what he asked; for he never asked for anything undeserved or unobtainable. Lewis correlates this enviable if improbable circumstance with one of George's remarks on prayer: "He who seeks the Father more than anything He can give, is likely to have what he asks, for he is not likely to ask amiss." Lewis adds that "the theological maxim is rooted in the experience of the author's childhood. This is what may be called the 'anti-Freudian predicament' in operation."[5] Robert Lee Wolff, on the other hand, who refuses to believe anything of the sort, remarks: "I leave to students of Lewis the job of explaining his triumphal assertion of MacDonald's freedom from Freud."[6] As an apostle of Freud, Wolff insists that MacDonald must have suffered from an involved sort of Oedipus complex, disturbed by the fact that MacDonald's mother died when he was eight. According to Wolff, the father could not substitute for the mother's tenderness, nor for her sexual attractiveness. Since nothing of this sort can, of course, be found in Greville MacDonald's biography, Wolff looks for confirmation in the novels and insists that he finds it everywhere. He proposes, without factual evidence, that MacDonald, unable to resolve his Oedipal wishes, nurtured a lifelong fantasy of sleeping with his mother.

At sixteen MacDonald entered a public school in Aberdeen, winning a bursary (scholarship) to the University of Aberdeen a year later, in 1840. At the university he embarked upon a scientific curriculum, but in 1842 he ran out of money and had to leave school to accumulate some savings. It is quite possible that the temporary rustication was due, in part at least, to some degree of overindulgence in alcohol and at the city's brothels, although again Greville MacDonald naturally does not discuss the question. But in *Alec Forbes of Howglen* (1865), a largely autobiographical novel, MacDonald clearly implies that his hero fell into a deplorable course of hinted-at vice while at the university.

Whatever the reason for MacDonald's leaving his studies in 1842, that summer one of the most important events of his life certainly occurred. According to Greville MacDonald, his father "spent some summer months in a certain castle or mansion in the far North, the locality of which I have failed to trace, in cataloguing a neglected library. . . . The library, wherever it was, and whatever its scope, added much to the materials upon which his imagination worked in future years."[7] While it is often unwise to interpret passages of ostensible fiction as autobiographical,

Greville MacDonald does not hesitate to cite from *The Portent*
(1864), one of his father's romances, a description of his experience in this northern library; the passage, which follows, is almost
certainly autobiographical: "I found a perfect set of our poets,
perfect according to the notion of the editor and the issue of the
publisher, although it omitted both Chaucer and George Herbert.
. . . But I found in the library what I liked far better, many
romances of a very marvellous sort, and plentiful interruption
they gave to the formation of the catalogue. I likewise came upon
a whole nest of the German classics . . . ; happening to be a tol-
erable reader of German, I found these volumes a mine of wealth
inexhaustible." [8]

The English poets, the literature of romance, the works of the
German Romantics—these are the most profound and permanent
influences upon MacDonald's own works. Together they set in
motion his change from an ordinary young Scotch scientist to a
religious mystic and votary of the imagination. As Lewis suggests,
the profound effect of this experience can be traced throughout
MacDonald's works: "The image of a great house seen principally
from the library and always through the eyes of a stranger or a
dependent (even Mr. Lane in *Lilith* never seems at home in the
library which is called his) haunts his books to the end. It is therefore reasonable to suppose that the 'great house in the North' was
the scene of some important crisis or development in his life." [9]

The same experience, whatever its nature, figures in the lives of
almost every protagonist in MacDonald's most autobiographical
novels; but no explicit account of what happened that summer
exists. Professor Wolff is sure that MacDonald must have fallen in
love with the daughter of the house but that she eventually
dropped him because she thought his social status inferior. Such
circumstances do appear now and then in the novels; but Wolff,
although he makes a plausible case, builds upon conjecture. Wolff
adds that this experience caused MacDonald to develop a permanent and neurotic hatred for rich noblemen, basing this conclusion upon the fact that aristocratic villains are found in most of
MacDonald's stories. Wolff conveniently chooses to ignore the
equally indisputable fact that upper-class villains are a staple of
Victorian fiction, often no doubt designed to appeal to a lower-
class reader's jealousy—a commercial consideration which Mac-
Donald, who needed the widest possible market, surely would not

ignore. In any case, MacDonald always depicts libraries as places of high excitement, sources of thrilling secrets, the settings for dramatic encounters between heroes and villains or for love scenes.

When MacDonald returned to the university in 1843, he entered a period of inward ferment and outward gloom, marked by religious doubts; and he also began writing Romantic poetry after the manner of Byron. His studies prospered and he received his master's degree in chemistry and in natural philosophy (physics) in 1845. Several years of indecision followed, during which MacDonald earned a meager living as a private tutor in Fulham, a district of southwest London. Several of his heroes, who also spend some years as tutors, usually undergo at the time spiritual crises. Precisely what inward struggles MacDonald went through we do not know, but he decided sometime in 1847 or 1848 to become a minister. Probably a good deal of his personal religion had been worked out by this date.

Also during this period he met Louisa Powell, to whom he became engaged in 1848; but they could not afford to marry. In the fall of 1848 MacDonald entered Highbury College, London, a struggling Congregationalist divinity school, to study for the ministry. Just after he graduated in 1850, new problems arose before he could take over his first parish in Arundel, Sussex. In December he was stricken with the first of his serious tubercular attacks; thereafter, his lungs troubled him. MacDonald's father died of a tubercular bone infection; his two beloved brothers succumbed while young; and the disease killed in childhood four of MacDonald's eleven children. In later years, he grimly referred to tuberculosis as "the family attendant."

While he was convalescing, difficulty arose between him and Louisa Powell. From Greville MacDonald's perhaps deliberately obscure account, Louisa resented the fact that the mystic considered earthly love as inferior and as perhaps contradictory to his love of God. Whatever the exact nature of the crisis, it led to his starting work on his first major literary attempt, a long dramatic poem entitled *Within and Without* (not published until 1855). The work, which presents an account of a love misunderstanding presumably similar to his own, displays most of the faults of his poetry—a smooth facility of versification combined with a lack of the vigor of expression found in his best fiction. Reading Mac-

Donald's poetry is often a pleasantly musical experience in which the reader has trouble remembering or caring about what has been said.

By the time MacDonald assumed the ministry of the church at Arundel in the spring of 1851, his trouble with Louisa was resolved, and the marriage took place. At about the same time came the first of his published works, a translation of *Twelve Spiritual Songs of Novalis*, which was privately printed in Edinburgh.[10] It is important to note that at this time MacDonald was only an occasional writer; he considered his true calling the ministry. Soon enough, however, he was forced to make literature his career, somewhat against his will.

In May, 1853, came the deciding crisis of George MacDonald's life. He was forced to resign his pulpit under pressure from his congregation, the elders of which resented his unorthodoxy. Presumably, they were shocked at his preaching that the heathen would be saved. Though suddenly unemployable in his profession, MacDonald felt that his vocation was genuinely a summons from God and, like Jonah's, inescapable. But he now had no money, and he had a wife and an infant daughter to support. This blow and his economic need, and his determined reaction to each, decided MacDonald's fate. He resolved to earn a living as a writer if he could and to incorporate into his works the urgent religious message which he felt called upon to disseminate, pulpit or no pulpit. For most of the rest of his life he had to live by writing, supplementing his slender income with whatever odd jobs and subsidies he could find. In addition to his literary work, he lectured, wrote hack reviews, edited a children's magazine while it lasted, and later was the impresario of dramatic performances acted by himself and his family.

MacDonald's literary career began painfully and slowly. Not until 1855 could he find a publisher for *Within and Without*, and the growing family's poverty meanwhile was extreme. But the poem's appearance promptly started him on the way to the reputation and popularity which he consolidated during the succeeding decade. Charles Kingsley wrote to him; Lady Byron, the poet's widow, became his friend and patron. She was a moral and religious uplifter and philanthropist; her gifts and bequests to the MacDonald family actually kept them from starvation until the father's writing began to produce an income of sorts.

Phantastes, his first prose book and the first of the symbolic works, appeared in 1858. It was generally ignored or abused, although several fairy stories of about the same time were better received. The first of MacDonald's conventional novels, *David Elginbrod,* was published in 1863 and immediately became celebrated for the epitaph of the hero's ancestor:

> Here lie I, Martin Elginbrodde:
> Hae mercy o' my soul, Lord God;
> As I wad do, were I Lord God,
> And ye were Martin Elginbrodde.

The rest of MacDonald's life is not so important to his fiction as his early years, for his religious and artistic consciousness never changed appreciably through the remaining decades of his life. Already in *Phantastes* and *David Elginbrod* he was a mystic of a sort, had worked out the tenets of his personal religion, and had displayed a mastery of symbolic technique scarcely equalled in his era. In realistic fiction he never needed to improve upon *David Elginbrod,* nor did he especially try. It was popular, it paid, it got its message across; its author was satisfied—no doubt too easily.

During the 1860's, *David Elginbrod* was followed by a rush of realistic novels in the same mode, usually but not always written partly in lowland Scots dialect. MacDonald's reputation, friendships, and family multiplied steadily. By 1872 he was sufficiently famous to capitalize upon his renown with a lecture tour in the United States. In thus following the example of Dickens, he netted over a thousand pounds. Meanwhile, MacDonald was befriended by John Ruskin and was intimately involved in Ruskin's strange love affair with Rose La Touche. For a time Rose lived with the MacDonald family, which was charged by her parents with the girl's protection. According to Greville MacDonald, his father even went so far as to interrogate the more famous man, including a frank question as to Ruskin's potency.[11]

In 1873 MacDonald was granted a civil list pension of one hundred pounds a year by Queen Victoria, and he acquired a residence at Bordighera in the Italian Riviera, where he wintered thereafter for the sake of his lungs. His novels, which continued to come out almost annually through the 1880's, were increasingly popular. From time to time, whenever he got far enough ahead of his bills to afford a sure failure, he indulged his less popular taste for fantasy, and he went on writing fairy tales for children which are still classics.

MacDonald became a close friend of "Lewis Carroll," who had his doubts about the value of *Alice in Wonderland* and tested it on the MacDonald children, accepting their favorable verdict before trying to publish it. Upon Tennyson's death in 1892, Mac-Donald was apparently considered for the laureateship on the basis of the considerable body of poetry which he had by then produced; but the idea never received very serious support, and the vacant post went to Alfred Austin—hardly a better poet than MacDonald.[12]

The frequency of MacDonald's publications understandably began to decline by 1890, when he was sixty-six years old. His last work, the story "Far Above Rubies," appeared in 1898. In 1897 MacDonald's chronic eczema became severe and damaged his health generally; in 1900 he apparently suffered a stroke and lost the power of speech. After a long illness George MacDonald died in 1905, leaving behind him a record of grim struggles, of the nobility with which he bore them, and of the reverence in which he was held by everyone who knew him.

III *A Family of Muses*

Although MacDonald's fiction was the basis both for his former fame and for what reputation he has in the twentieth century, we should mention his works in other literary genres. A prolific man of letters, he wrote in nearly every imaginable form—poetry, essays, criticism, closet drama, hackwork, editing, translation, and so forth. The poetry is usually fluent and melodious, but only occasionally does MacDonald achieve in verse the force and distinction of his best narrative prose. Perhaps he was *too* facile as a versifier: his lines are smooth but slack and wordy. He repeatedly revised his verses for successive republications, with the usual results—very little improvement, if any. An edition of *The Poetical Works of George MacDonald* was published in 1893.

MacDonald's criticism and reviews are likewise undistin-guished, although an essay on Shelley was incorporated into the eighth edition of the *Encyclopaedia Britannica* (1860). One of his most curious productions was a critical edition of *Hamlet* from the first folio text, in which he argued fiercely that the prince is too

Christian to contemplate suicide seriously. I have been told that Sir John Gielgud bases his reading of the role upon MacDonald's edition. MacDonald argued that the Prince of Denmark is unlike the usual tragic hero in that he is essentially without a real flaw; he is neither insane, nor tempted to commit suicide, nor unduly hesitant, but rather a reverent Christian who honestly fears that the ghost may be a delusive snare of the devil. Thus, Hamlet must be very careful not to fall into a trap; he must assure himself that it is really the ghost of his father before assuming the role of a just avenger.

More interesting and relevant to this study are MacDonald's many translations, most of which appeared together in an obscurely titled volume, *Rampolli: growths from a long-planted root* (1897). He was fond of Dante and of the German Romantics; his renderings of Novalis (the pen name of Friedrich von Hardenburg) are possibly the best in English, illustrating the profound influence of that earlier mystic.

But the most important works, aside from the fiction, are the several volumes of sermons and the single volume of personal essays in which MacDonald set forth many of the original and striking ideas which his stories illustrate and embody. Chapter 2 of this study concentrates upon these works and upon the philosophy (or theology) which they express.

For the present, the fiction must be the chief subject of any study of MacDonald. The idea of classifying literature into genera, species, and subspecies, as if one were a biological taxonomist, is perhaps rather risky; for the analogy between types of organism and types of literature is far from dependable. But the crucial distinction between realistic and fantastic fiction must at least be strongly emphasized. These two kinds of storytelling require entirely different talents—even different prose styles. They likewise appeal to different tastes, so that the distinction between them is important for what it may show about the course of literary history. Furthermore, the fact that MacDonald deliberately sought to use literature as a pulpit raises the question of whether realistic or fantastic fiction is better suited, inherently, for didactic purposes.

By "realism" I mean not the creation of a completely credible world like the one in which we live, work, and suffer, but an attempt in that direction. Certainly MacDonald's conventional novels are at times Gothic, sensational, and incredible, but those are faults in the execution, not in the conception, which at least *aims* at a sense of possibility. The imaginative or fantastic works (I shall use the terms interchangeably), by contrast, make no attempt at mere feasibility; they are created rather than re-created. The distinction may be conveniently if incompletely drawn in terms of the presence or absence of the supernatural: the fantasies are filled with ghosts and spirits, witches and demons, fiends and fairies, talking animals and sentient plants.

Even by drawing such a line, I find some works difficult to classify. The children's story *At the Back of the North Wind* (1871), for example, owes much of its effectiveness to its grim portrayal of poor people's lives in an all-too-real London; but, because the realistic narrative is interrupted by several journeys into the Other World, I place it among the fantasies. Despite such difficulties of classification, the realistic-fantastic dichotomy proves, I believe, to be both real and instructive.

The realistic works include a number of sentimental short stories, but these are vastly outweighed by twenty-nine conventional novels, most of them written in the sentimental Victorian tradition, happy ending and all. One is a Horatio Alger inspirational story for children, *Gutta Percha Willie* (1873); another, a historical novel of Cavaliers and Roundheads, *St. George and St. Michael* (1876); eleven are largely in lowland Scots dialect; and the rest, Edifying Exampla of Proper Victorian Behavior, are the works which sold best in MacDonald's lifetime; and they are, in the light of history, the ones most assured of permanent and deserved oblivion.

The imaginative stories are more likely to achieve permanence —or so it may be hoped. Even when MacDonald neglects the symbolic suggestiveness which was his major gift, he displays one of the most fecund visionary faculties in literature. He was endlessly capable of inventing worlds of excitement, charm, and beauty, and of reminding many readers of the tantalizing, unrecapturable aura of lovely dreams. The full-length children's stories *The Princess and the Goblin* (1872), *The Princess and Curdie* (1883), *A Double Story* (as a serial, 1874–75), and *At the Back of the North Wind,* are classics to some degree. In addition, there are a number of delightful shorter fairy tales, of which "The Light Princess" and "The Golden Key" are the finest. (It was from the latter that Wolff got the title for his study of MacDonald's fiction.)

It is generally conceded by the few modern critics interested in MacDonald that his finest works are the symbolic fantasies for adults. In these he has adapted many of the conventions and devices of the fairy story to works for grownups, as he indicated in the subtitle of his first such work, *Phantastes: A Faerie Romance for Men and Women*. Even finer in its excitement, symbolic resonance, and psychological truth is *Lilith* (1895), which is probably MacDonald's masterpiece. There is a third volume which might be classified with these two—*The Portent*—but which I place in an intermediate category because its setting is entirely earthly and its apparently supernatural elements may more properly be called superstitious. Some of MacDonald's most striking imaginative works are short fantasies for adults, often focusing more closely upon the same symbols found in the visionary novels.

In the chapters which follow, I examine all of the stories, both realistic and fantastic, although I deal with some of them collectively rather than one at a time. In the process, I concentrate upon three general aims. First, I review MacDonald's ideas, not because I consider them a vital and neglected message—though they are interesting and striking enough—but to identify the currents of his thought for the purpose of illuminating *how* he embodied that thought in fiction. In dealing with a less consciously didactic writer, such material would be less important for appreciating his works, but with MacDonald it is practically indispensable: MacDonald developed his views early, *before* the loss of his pulpit forced him to attempt their expression in fiction; therefore, I follow the same course and devote my second chapter to his "philosophy," *before* treating its fictional embodiment.

Further, I attempt to place MacDonald in the context of literary history. Obviously, he spoke effectively to his contemporaries, especially through his conventional novels; yet the fact that he is nearly forgotten today suggests that his realistic works, at least, are inappropriate in a new era of taste and world outlook. We may, indeed, suspect that there was something characteristically "Victorian" about him, something which the twentieth century has discarded, rightly or wrongly—and that quality may account both for his former reputation and for his recent neglect. As for the symbolic works, why is it that they were ignored during their author's lifetime but have become the cornerstone of whatever reputation he has now and, presumably, will have in the future? I shall try to demonstrate that an examination of MacDonald's works can tell us a great deal about the time in which he wrote them and about the age that followed. After all, the shifts in literary tastes are the touchstone of literary history and perhaps provide a clue to history in general.

The symbolic fantasies have undergone a distinct upgrading in critical favor. There seems to be something in the twentieth-century sensibility which values metaphysical, religious, and psychological symbolism as a way of expressing the fundamentals of human existence—something which the Victorian era apparently cared little for, judging from the fact that MacDonald was one of the few Victorian writers who wrote works of that kind. As C. S. Lewis points out, in the shrewdest remark on MacDonald which I have seen, "A dominant form tends to attract to itself writers whose talents would have fitted them much better for work of some other kind. Thus the retiring Cowper writes satire in the eighteenth century; or in the nineteenth a mystic and natural symbolist like George MacDonald is seduced into writing novels." [13]

Third, possibly the most important of my objectives is critical and even theoretical. I can think of very few writers who achieved some distinction in both realistic and fantastic literature. The coincidence of the two apparently incompatible forms in the works of one author provides an ideal laboratory setting for exploring the nature of, and the differences between, the novel and the fantasy, the invented history and the invented myth. Furthermore, since MacDonald had the same general didactic purposes in mind whatever he wrote, he offers an opportunity to study the different ways in which the same "message" may be conveyed. If symbolically, how are the symbols found and why are they effective? If dramatically in a realistic context, how are the conflicts established? And if in straightforward, declarative didacticism after the manner of G. B. Shaw's dramas, what effect does the inclusion of such expository material have upon the novel form?

CHAPTER 2

MacDonald's Ideas

I *The Novelist as Philosopher, or Vice Versa*

ALTHOUGH I am not engaged in the propagation of George MacDonald's ideas as such, MacDonald's philosophy is, for one thing, the very foundation upon which his works of fiction are laid. Most writers of fiction, perhaps, are chiefly interested in telling a good story with skill, discipline, and art—such are Jane Austen and Henry James, for example. But there have been plenty of great writers, such as Dostoevsky and Shaw, to whom their private vision of Truth is primary, and who use their art as a means to expression of that end; and MacDonald belongs clearly with this group.

Furthermore, MacDonald's ideas are sometimes striking, often profound, usually logical, and almost always interesting in themselves, quite aside from how they are embodied. Lewis's *George MacDonald: An Anthology* and Greville MacDonald's biography both make some progress toward treating MacDonald's religious philosophy systematically, but neither attempt goes very far. Although MacDonald himself never really put forward his ideas as a coherent system, a close examination of his scattered philosophical remarks has convinced me that they all arise from a systematic, consistent set of beliefs.

As I have already suggested, MacDonald's characteristic and most effective mode of intellectual or philosophical expression is through the suggestive, poetic, and impalpable language of symbol and myth. Rather than "decoding" the symbols to arrive at a declarative formulation of their meaning, however, we begin with MacDonald's direct statements, as they appear here and there in his works, before undertaking an analysis of their symbolic or dramatic embodiment. This chapter relies chiefly, therefore, upon MacDonald's works which are expository rather than fictional in nature, although passages are cited from the fictional works where

MacDonald attributes his own views to characters invented chiefly for this purpose.

The most important expository works are the several volumes of sermons and religious essays: *The Miracles of Our Lord* (1870), *Unspoken Sermons* (1867), *Unspoken Sermons: Second Series* (1885), *Unspoken Sermons: Third Series* (1889), and *The Hope of the Gospel* (1892). The term "unspoken sermons," incidentally, indicates MacDonald's lifelong preoccupation with the fact that he had no pulpit from which to deliver his message. Each of these books consists of a dozen or so interlinked chapters devoted to various biblical texts or incidents, after the traditional fashion of sermons. Besides these specifically religious volumes, there is a collection of essays, mostly secular, with the unfortunate title of *A Dish of Orts* (1893). This miscellany concentrates largely upon literary criticism and theory, with a sermon and a couple of essays in psychology included.[1]

For the sake of convenience, MacDonald's thought may be sub-divided into four areas of greatest interest and emphasis, although his incidental remarks are inclined to range over whatever other topics may interest him at the moment; for, like any sage worthy of the title, MacDonald was willing to pronounce upon anything, anywhere. These four areas are religion, psychology, social and political matters, and literary theory, all of which are important to an understanding of his fiction.

II *Theology: Heretic, Prophet, Mystic*

In religious matters, as I have pointed out, MacDonald was thoroughly unorthodox and even heretically eccentric. His theology shows a good deal of eclecticism (a horrid word to conventional religious thinkers as it is to many literary critics), but much of it seems entirely original and personal; and it must be regarded as a private religion which to MacDonald was distinctly Christian—but so was that of William Blake, whom he admired. MacDonald was associated with F. D. Maurice, leader of the "broad church" movement which sought to incorporate and leave room for a broad range of doctrine within the body of the Anglican establishment. Maurice's influence even led MacDonald to join the English church eventually, although he dissented from a good many of the Thirty-nine Articles. He certainly belonged to the "liberal" faction, neither High nor Low, which, with the so-called higher critics, believed that the Bible is a historical document written by fallible men who were quite capable of unwitting distortions and misrepresentations of the words of Jesus and that many biblical passages must be taken figuratively rather than literally.

Often MacDonald's peculiar views led him into what orthodox or sectarian Christians consider outright heresy. In addition, a strong infusion of mysticism in his outlook led him to flirt with the uncomfortable but incontrovertible position of the typical mystic that he has received knowledge through inspiration, directly from God, including insights which had been "left out" of the Bible. MacDonald apparently read widely in the classic literature of mysticism, including Swedenborg and Boehme as well as the Christian saints. He also read some of Blake but probably not the prophetic books, which were hard to find in the late nineteenth century. I have, unfortunately, been quite unable to discover which books were in MacDonald's library; and I presume that it was scattered upon his death.[2] Despite the eclecticism of MacDonald's religious philosophy, it seems to be remarkably logical and consistent. It should be pointed out, however, that he never formulated it in any particularly systematic fashion and that, in imposing a certain coherence upon his ideas, I may be guilty of some distortion. With this awareness, we may examine his specific doctrines.

During his youth, MacDonald confronted the harsh Calvinism of his native Scotland and found it repulsive. He refused to believe that God could be so "unfair" as to condemn anyone in advance. In rejecting the doctrine of the elect, he was fond of insisting "I did not care for God to love me if He did not love everybody."[3] Having thus questioned the doctrine accepted by his Aberdeenshire neighbors, he approached every religious doctrine with the same skepticism, always based upon the idea of God's *fairness*. The inquiry led him to confront all of the usual problems of Christianity from a peculiar angle: how could God fulfill his attributes of infinite justice *and* infinite mercy together, without contradiction or unfairness—for surely God must be infinitely more fair and equitable than even the most perfect man. Thus, a man might speculatively apply his own human standards of "fair-

ness" to such questions as the punishment of sin and the rewarding of virtue and be assured that God would be even fairer than
he himself could dream of being.

After years of search, MacDonald presumably discovered one
central principle which enabled him to resolve every contradiction, to deny every shortcoming of this world of pain and trouble,
to rationalize the optimism of his instincts. This central insight has
to do with the idea that, in dealing with His creatures, God must
descend from His timelessness into the temporal world, since all
creatures, unlike their creator, exist in time. "That God could not
do the thing at once which he takes time to do, we may surely say
without irreverence." "God is limited by regard for our best; our
best implies education; in this we ourselves must have a large
share; this share, being human, involves time." And, referring to
Jesus's curing of the sick; MacDonald pondered: "Why then did
he not cure all the sick in Judea? Simply because all were not
ready to be cured. . . . Their illness had not yet wrought its
work, had not yet ripened them to the possibility of faith; his cure
would have left them deeper in evil than before." [4]

Coupled with the idea that God's work takes time is the postulate that His intentions toward His creatures are, ultimately, completely and infinitely benevolent—that He expects every inferior
being to attain eventual perfection. These axioms, when carried to
their inevitable logical conclusion, lead to a number of fascinating
deductions. For one thing, they enable MacDonald to resolve, to
his own satisfaction at least, the problem of evil! "What if all was
right in the heart of things,—right, even as a man, if he could
understand, would say was right; right, so that a man who understood a part could believe it to be ten times more right than he did
understand!" "What we call evil is only the best shape, which, for
the person and his condition *at the time,* could be assumed by the
best good." "Evil, that is physical evil, is a moral good—a mighty
means to a lofty end." "In those who believe that good is the one
power, and that evil exists only because *for a time* it subserves,
cannot help subserving the good, what place can there be for
fear?" [5]

Such optimism is likely to strike the modern reader as deplor-
ably typical of the smugness which we, in our own smugness,
ascribe to the Victorians; but the case is more complicated than it
appears. The temper of the eighteenth century had lent itself to

something similar—Pope's "Whatever is, is right" and the Leibnit-
zian doctrine that this is the best of all possible worlds—but toward the end of that century the question had been reopened by
the disastrous and gratuitous Lisbon earthquake (1755), which
killed thousands on a Sunday morning while they prayed. After
that experience, and after Voltaire's *Candide* had apparently laid
philosophical optimism to rest, no literate Victorian could lightly
assert the infinite benevolence of God. MacDonald's adoption of
this view was neither glib nor naïve; he knew, if anyone did, that
the world's suffering is bitter enough. The idea, therefore, of re-
solving the problem by presenting it as a consequence of God's
limitation in time, when He deals with this world and its people,
is a subtle, almost existential synthesis.

Physical evil, then, is God's way of educating man, through a
period of time, with the end in view of perfecting him; but man's
achievement of perfection may be limited by man's own temporal
condition. Thus, a man who dies unregenerate or ignorant will
receive in the next world the educating punishment which he
missed in this one, but each man's *ultimate* end is perfection. "I
believe that no hell will be lacking which would help the just
mercy of God redeem his children." "God loves where he cannot yet forgive—where forgiveness in the full sense is as yet simply impossible, because no contact of hearts is possible, because
that which lies between has not even begun to yield to the besom
of his holy destruction." [6]

The means by which man is brought by God to redemption are
through punishment, in this world or in a future hell, that requires
in most cases a period of time and that culminates in man's recognition of his own depravity. But, once this insight is attained, the
road to salvation is clear; thus, a sinner's stay in hell is *not* permanent, though it may be long. "For the man who in this world re-
sists to the full, there may be, perhaps, a whole age or era in the
history of the universe during which his sin shall not be forgiven;
but *never* can it be forgiven until he repents." "The one deepest,
highest, truest, fittest, most wholesome suffering must be generated in the wicked by a vision, a true sight, of the hideousness of
their lives, of the horror of the wrongs they have done." But "The
notion that a creature born imperfect, nay, born with impulses to
evil not of his own generating, and which he could not help having, a creature to whom the true face of God was never presented,

and by whom it never could have been seen, should be eternally condemned, is as loathesome a lie against God as could find a place in a heart too undeveloped to understand what justice is." [7]

In a short story about an idiot, MacDonald speculates this way about his character's afterlife: "He was like a seed buried too deep in the soil, to which the light has never penetrated, and which, therefore, has never forced its way upward to the open air, never experienced the resurrection of the dead. But seeds will grow ages after they have fallen into the earth; and, indeed, with many kinds, and within some limits, the older the seed before it germinates, the more plentiful is the fruit. And may it not be believed of many human beings, that, the great Husbandman having sown them like seeds sown in the soil of human affairs, there they lie buried a life long; and, only after the up-turning of the soil by death, reach the position in which the awakening of aspiration and the consequent growth become possible. Surely he has made nothing in vain." [8]

One consequence of this line of thought is that MacDonald found himself espousing several traditional "heresies." Obviously, for instance, the eternal damnation of unbaptized infants strikes MacDonald as "unfair"—as it must have appeared to any number of thoughtful Christians. Likewise, the heathen who have never heard of Christ's message will have another chance in the afterlife; and this doctrine probably resulted in MacDonald's dismissal by his parish. Even the recalcitrant, unregenerate sinner gets another chance—as many chances as are needed to bring him to repentance. Finally, even Satan will come to repentance and thus to the possibility of redemption—the ultimate heresy, I suppose. But this last consequence of his postulates was too bold for Mac-Donald to risk its direct assertion. Rather, he contents himself with putting the thought into the mouths of his fictional characters merely as speculation, from which their inventor could safely dissociate himself. For example, in *Robert Falconer* (1868), that most sympathetic of his heroes presents the idea to his closest friend this way: " 'Shargar, what think ye?' he said suddenly, one day. 'Gin a de'il war to repent, wad God forgie him?' 'There's no sayin' what folk wad du ance they're tried,' returned Shargar, cautiously." [9]

The tone of speculation in this quotation should not go unremarked. MacDonald admits that this world *seems* unjust and that nobody has seen the hypothetical posthumous world(s) on the other side of death and lived to describe them, but he argues that the demands of eventual justice *must* be met after death if the work is uncompleted in this world. Upon the nature of this truer world after death, he may legitimately speculate: "Why should I not speculate in the only direction in which things worthy of speculation appear likely to lie? There is a wide *may be* around us; and every true speculation widens the probability of changing the *may be* into the *is*." [10]

Here we approach another aspect of MacDonald's religious thought. Even if problems of evil and punishment, justice and mercy, sin and damnation have been resolved, we are still faced with the question of what we can understand and *do* toward salvation in *this* life, since that is clearly our business. And, if the world on the other side of death is truer than this one, how can we anticipate its truth in order to hasten the temporal process of salvation? In short, if we are to be educated in the course of time, how can we accelerate that education?

MacDonald's answer to the problem of *how* we are to "educate" ourselves in this life is that of the typical Christian mystic. He pictures God not only as transcendent in his inconceivable perfection but also as immanent in this world. He has provided us with what we need for our education, if only we will look for it. God's will and nature are expressed throughout His creation. Through the proper use of insight, we can learn even while subjected to the limitations and imperfections of our earthly existence. MacDonald finds three potential sources of such mystical insight: in the biblical deeds and sayings of Jesus, in Nature, and in Man himself.

I shall not discuss at much length MacDonald's theories about the interpretation of Christ's words in the New Testament, because his views are essentially those of every other interpreter—that Jesus taught precisely what the interpreter believed all along. The Calvinists too, after all, can ingeniously find support for their ideas in the words of Jesus, thus perhaps showing more about Calvinists than about Jesus. Furthermore, whenever Jesus is reported to have said something which MacDonald could not accept, he suggests that the Savior has been misquoted. Nevertheless, the words of Jesus are truths, or metaphorically have truths behind them. It is up to us to read the New Testament with sympathy and insight, but we must keep in mind two things: first, that

the Bible is, according to the Higher Criticism popular in Mac-
Donald's time, the report of fallible and limited men; and, second,
that Jesus was, after all, the son of God, and could therefore not
be expected to see things in limited human terms. Referring to the
characteristic mode of expression of Jesus, practiced and perhaps
consciously imitated by MacDonald himself, he remarks that "The
Lord puts things in subdefined, suggestive shapes, yielding no sat-
isfactory meaning to the mere intellect. . . . According as the
new creation, that of reality, advances in him, the man becomes
able to understand the words, the symbols, the parables of the
Lord." [11]

More interesting, and more productive for the purposes of critical analysis, are MacDonald's views on God's self-expression in
nature. "This world is not merely a thing which God hath made,
subjecting it to laws; but it is an expression of the thought, the
feeling, the heart of God himself." "Nature is brimful of symbolic and analogical parallels to the goings and comings, the
growth and changes of the highest nature in man." "The faces of
some flowers lead me back to the heart of God; and, as his child, I
hope I feel, in my lowly degree, what he felt when, brooding over
them, he said 'They are good'; that is, 'They are what I mean.'"
"There is not a form that lives in the world, but is a window
cloven through the blank darkness of nothingness, to let us look
into the heart, and feeling, and nature of God." [12]

MacDonald's idea that everything in nature is an expression of
God's thought reminds one inevitably of the language of the mystics—of, for instance, Emanuel Swedenborg: "The whole natural world corresponds to the spiritual world, and not merely the
natural world in general, but also every particular of it." Or of
Jacob Boehme: "The spiritual world is hidden within the visible
elementary world, and acts through the latter. . . . It shapes itself in all things according to the nature and quality of each
thing." William Law: "Everything in temporal nature is descended out of that which is eternal, and stands as a palpable
visible outbirth of it." [13] However, the existence of a single such
agreement between MacDonald and any other mystic proves
nothing by itself; the important point is that *all* mystics exhibit
many psychological attributes and metaphysical ideas in common,
as Evelyn Underhill has richly demonstrated in her classic study,
Mysticism. Of these typically mystical attributes, MacDonald dis-

plays a great number—enough to warrant his inclusion among that curious group of similar men collectively called "mystic personalities." Underhill makes it clear, though perhaps she did not mean to, that the term "mystic" refers to a psychological type, a way of seeing things, a characteristic mode of behavior, as do such terms as "hysteric" or "manic-depressive."

It is here, in fact, that any arbitrary distinction between MacDonald's religious and psychological thought tends to break down. For as soon as we begin to discuss (after Jesus and Nature) the third source of knowledge about God and truth, man's own heart, we are involved equally in religion and psychology. George MacDonald was no pure scientist, interested in empirical knowledge for its own sake. He was fascinated by the mysteries of the human mind because he believed it a legitimate source of religious rather than "merely" scientific truth. Therefore, in discussing his psychological thought, I make no great effort to distinguish painstakingly between psychology and religion.

MacDonald himself seems to have recognized that the mystic personality is a distinct type, although his few remarks on the subject are devoted to only a sampling of the type's attributes. He explicitly remarks upon the concept of nature's correspondence with spiritual truth in this context:

I use the word *mysticism* as representing a certain mode of embodying the truth, common, in various degrees, to almost all, if not all, the writers of the New Testament. The attempt to define it thoroughly would require an essay. I will hazard but one suggestion towards it: A mystical mind is one which, having perceived that the highest expression, of which truth admits, lies in the symbolism of nature, and the human customs which result from human necessities, prosecutes thought about truth so embodied by dealing with the symbols themselves after logical forms.[14]

It is, perhaps, unfortunate that MacDonald never wrote that essay; but this passage makes it clear that he understood something of what Evelyn Underhill subsequently formulated in *Mysticism*. In a remarkable essay entitled "A Sketch of Individual Development," MacDonald carefully traced the stages through which a mystic passes in the course of his spiritual education. The picture he draws is just what Miss Underhill finds in all mystics, and it clearly describes each of what she called the five steps along the "mystic way": (1) Awakening or Conversion, (2) Self-knowledge or Purgation, (3) Illumination, (4) Surrender or the Dark Night, (5) Union.[15]

MacDonald likewise describes, in his fiction especially, what is perhaps the most typical characteristic of mystical consciousness —the so-called mystic experience. This term is used to describe the moment of ecstatic insight into and identification with God which all true mystics report; and I must confess that, not having had such an experience myself, I can only guess at its nature on the basis of many accounts of such experiences which I have read. The authors of such accounts always find language a poor instrument for describing this elevated state, and that very dissatisfaction is one of the "signs" of a mystic experience's genuineness. MacDonald, who feels this limitation, warns his reader of the difficulty:

> In telling my—neither vision nor dream nor ecstasy, I cannot help it that the forms grow so much plainer and more definite in the words than they were in the revelation. Words always give either too much or too little shape: when you want to be definite, you find your words clumsy and blunt; when you want them for a vague shadowy image, you straightway find them giving a sharp and impertinent outline. . . . Forms themselves are hard enough to manage, but words are unmanageable. I must therefore trust to the heart of my reader.
>
> I crept into the bosom of God, and along a great cloudy peace, which I could not understand, for it did not yet enter into me. At length I came to the heart of God, and through that my journey lay. The moment I entered it, the great peace appeared to enter mine, and I began to understand it. . . . I had left myself behind in the heart of God, and now I was pure essence, fit to rejoice in the essential.[16]

One of MacDonald's most useful concepts with regard to the mystic way provides a clear connection—unfortunately lacking in many mystical philosophers—between metaphysical knowledge and moral action. In other words, MacDonald's religious-psychological ruminations contain an ethic of action. The key to MacDonald's ethic is what I call *the stepwise process of education in time*. He recognizes that man begins from ignorance and does not at first possess the necessary insight which would enable him to understand God's message, whether in the Gospel, in Nature, or in Man's own heart. The problem, then, is to gain such insight, which in turn will enable man to gain the knowledge which God has hidden in this world for his discovery. MacDonald's solution to the ethical problem is perhaps the most frequently reiterated of his categorical imperatives; it might be paraphrased as follows: "No matter how limited man's knowledge, he should *do* that which he knows to be right, and in the process he will learn to see more than he did at first." Or, to put it as does Carlyle, from whom MacDonald surely adopted the precept: "*Do the Duty which lies nearest thee,* which thou knowest to be a Duty! Thy second Duty will already have become clearer." In speaking of one of his untutored fictional saints, for instance, MacDonald characterizes him this way: "The main secret of his progress, the secret of all wisdom, was, that with him action was the beginning and end of thought." Again, "The rare thing is not the man who knows what is right, but the man who actually, with all the power in him, with his very being, sets himself to *do* that right thing." [17]

III   *Psychology: Freudian before Freud*

In addition to this partial analysis of the mystic personality which he himself displayed, MacDonald devoted great attention to the study of all aspects of the personality, especially to the submerged and hidden regions of the heart—the regions which Freud would later call the unconscious. Although MacDonald's anticipation of the Freudian concept of the unconscious is perhaps impressive, it is, of course, hardly unique. Indeed, Freud cheerfully admitted that "the poets" had perceived it before he did. Furthermore, many of the ideas which Freud developed and systematized were, in fragmentary form, already current in late nineteenth-century thought, with which MacDonald may well have been quite familiar. Robert Lee Wolff in *The Golden Key,* treats MacDonald's works as if they were unintentional revelations of their author's psychic troubles, but MacDonald knew much more about himself and about the nature of the mind than Wolff gives him credit for.

MacDonald's characteristic metaphor for the unknown regions of the mind is to picture them as hidden rooms in an unexplored building: "A house looks always to me so like a mind—full of strange inexplicable shapes at first sight, which gradually arrange, disentangle, and explain themselves as you go on to know them. Then in all houses, there are places we know nothing about as yet, or have but a vague idea or feeling of their existence—just as in our own selves, who carry in us deeper mysteries far than any we can suspect in another." [18]

These unexplored regions of the mind are, like the symbols of nature, a source of truth, since they are God's, not merely ours: "If the dark portion of our own being were the origin of our own imaginations, we might well fear the apparition of such monsters as would be generated in the sickness of a decay which could never feel—only declare—a slow return towards primeval chaos. But the Maker is our light." And, when speaking of artistic creation of new and original "forms" (a favorite and annoyingly vague word of MacDonald's), MacDonald asserts that "Such embodiments are not the result of the man's intention, or of the operation of his conscious nature. . . . But can we not say that they are the creation of the unconscious portion of his nature? . . . From that unknown region we grant they come, but not by its own blind working. . . . But God sits in that chamber of our being in which the candle of our consciousness goes out in darkness." [19]

Here is a clear anticipation of the Freudian picture of the unconscious, but modified by the idea that the unconscious, like nature, is a dwelling place of God, a source of spiritual truth. This is not to say, however, that MacDonald considered the unconscious to be exclusively of transcendent origin. He also suggested mechanisms by which once-conscious experience might be "forgotten" by the conscious mind and incorporated into the submerged unconscious—in short, MacDonald anticipated the Freudian concept of repression, along with the idea that repressed unpleasant memories may haunt one with guilt feelings of unrecognized origin:

The father of him sat staring at nothing, neither asleep nor awake, not quite lost in stupidity either, for through it all he was dimly angry with himself, he did not know why. It was that he had struck his wife. He had forgotten it, but was miserable about it, notwithstanding.

Never seeking true or high things, caring only for appearances and, therefore, for inventions, he had left his imagination all undeveloped, and when it represented his own inner condition to him, had repressed it until it was nearly destroyed, and what remained of it was set on fire of hell.[20]

MacDonald even suggests, at one point, the idea of prenatal memory which has figured among the most fantastic but plausible concepts of twentieth-century psychology: "If you can imagine a growing fruit, all blind and deaf, yet loving the tree it could neither look upon nor hear, knowing it only through the unbroken arrival of its life therefrom—that is something like what I felt. I suspect the *form* of the feeling was supplied by a shadowy memory of the time before I was born, while yet my life grew upon the life of my mother." [21]

Again like Freud, MacDonald attributed great importance to dreams as a direct pathway to the unconscious, a means of finding out the secrets which God has hidden there: "I believe that, if there be a living, conscious love at the heart of the universe, the mind, in the quiescence of its consciousness in sleep, comes into a less disturbed contact with its origin, the heart of creation." Dream images, in fact, contain hints of what the afterlife may be like—intimations of the nature of the "truer world" about which MacDonald believes it legitimate to speculate:

All dreams are not false; some dreams are truer than the plainest facts. Fact at best is but a garment of truth, which has ten thousand changes of raiment woven on the same loom. Let the dreamer only do the truth of his dream, and one day he will realize all that was worth realizing in it.

Some dreams . . . arouse individual states of consciousness altogether different from any of our waking moods, and not to be recalled by any mere effort of the will. . . . For I believe that those new, mysterious feelings that come to us in sleep . . . are indications of wells of feeling and delight which have not yet broken out of their hiding-place in our souls.[22]

As still another instance of MacDonald's remarkable anticipation of twentieth-century psychology, I refer again to "A Sketch of Individual Development." Although the individual in question is surely not typical of mankind, representing rather the peculiar mystical type (probably MacDonald himself), yet many of this hypothetical person's experiences are those of all of us. In the course of the first few pages, he describes the steps by which a newborn child acquires consciousness and a psychic topography. This astonishing work deserves to be quoted at length, but I can give only a few excerpts which may indicate the extent to which MacDonald may be called a true psychologist:

> By degrees he has learned that the world is around, and not within him—that he is apart, and that it is apart; from consciousness he passes to self-consciousness. . . . To a being weighted with a strong faculty for mistake, begins to be revealed the existence . . . of Being other and higher than his own, recognized as *Will*, and first of all in its opposition to his desires. . . . The first opposing glance of the mother wakes in the child not only answering opposition, . . . but a new something, to which for long he needs no name, so natural does it seem. . . . This new something—we call it *Conscience*—sides with his mother. . . . And now he not only knows, not only knows that he knows, but knows he knows that he knows—knows that he is self-conscious—that he has a conscience. . . . And here, even at this early point in his history, what I call his fourth birth *may* begin to take place: I mean the birth in him of the Will—the real Will—not the pseudo-will, which is mere Desire, swayed of impulse, selfishness, or one of many a miserable motive.[23]

Here we have, in fact, a concept of the compartmented personality, subdivided into conflicting elements directly comparable to Freud's ego ("self-consciousness"), superego ("conscience" or perhaps the "real Will"), and id ("mere Desire"). The fact that our language has always contained such words as "conscience" does not deprive Freud of his claim to having made a discovery, for Freud looked more deeply into such phenomena as the "conscience" and found therein a *mechanism* and a *causality* which had escaped earlier users of the word. Wordsworth, for instance, called Duty "stern daughter of the voice of God," a mixed metaphor which is both bad poetry and bad science. MacDonald's approach, through tracing the earliest experiences of any child, resembles Freud's (unlike Wordsworth's) in identifying the conscience-superego with the voice not of God but of the parent.

Finally, of course, and perhaps inevitably, mention must be made of MacDonald's view of sexuality as a powerful psychic vector. Unfortunately, this is the single important area of his interests about which he wrote nothing declarative and expository, in the sense that the passages cited so far in this chapter are examples of straightforward statement rather than of fictional dramatization or of symbolic embodiment. He repeatedly deals, however, with sex in symbolical or allegorical terms, but he does so in such a manner that no reader can doubt his consciousness of what he was doing. (Or perhaps I should say *almost* no reader. Professor Wolff evidently believes that MacDonald, like many of his contemporaries, was largely unaware of the sexual undertones in his own works and that in this respect he is a classic example of the Victorian "repression" of sexuality.) In MacDonald's fictional treatments of sexual motifs, he deliberately disguised his dramatizations of sexuality in deference to the prudery of the time. Indeed, MacDonald may have enjoyed concealing from the less sophisticated of his readers what he was really talking about.

IV   *The Social Conscience of an Aristocrat*

Unlike MacDonald's religious ideas and mystical psychology, his political and social theories were stubbornly unamenable to symbolic representation. He was affected by the social ferment of his age, by its materialism, and by its horrifying economic inequities which were so vividly depicted by Dickens. But at the same time, there is an annoying condescension about MacDonald; he seems to accept without question the very class structure which was largely responsible for the injustices of his time. He accepted on faith the conventional concepts of "good family" and "good blood," perhaps because he prided himself on his descent from the aristocratic Clan MacDonald.

This is not to say that MacDonald was insensitive to the problems of the working class. Although he did not recognize the existence of the industrial mass-proletariat, he was convinced that the individual artisan—the shoemaker, blacksmith, carpenter, mason—was the backbone of the English social and economic system. No doubt he was influenced by the social theories of Ruskin and William Morris, who longed for the vanished day of the individual workman's dignity before he was engulfed by mass production and wage slavery; for MacDonald's scattered suggestions toward utopia are usually built along the lines of medieval feudalism. He did not question the right of landlords to own immense acreages, but he did insist that their exalted status carried with it an obligation to their tenants and to the land itself, which should be kept in good order. As we shall see in the next chapter, such romantic, embryonic, derivative, and rather simple-minded social schemes recur in many of the realistic novels and account for a good deal of their banality. Because of this simplicity and unoriginality, it is hardly necessary to illustrate MacDonald's social views with profuse quotations, as in the case of his more subtle religious and psychological concepts.

One other aspect of MacDonald's social thought deserves some attention, however. His moral philosophy of action—actually *doing* that which man sees to be right, however limited his insight— led him to consider what a man's duty was with regard to the suffering and degradation of the masses. His conclusion was that man must *minister* to them—a moral imperative no doubt connected with a literal interpretation of his Christian principles. The desire to serve the unfortunate led MacDonald into the movement of "social work" which was just beginning around the middle of the nineteenth century to assume its present aspect. This interest brought him into contact with Octavia Hill, the pioneer English social worker, who became his close friend and who was the model for several of his heroines. But again the irritating condescension appears: MacDonald's social workers customarily operate *de haut en bas*. Nevertheless, MacDonald probably played some significant part in the formation of the Victorian social conscience, the ancestor of our own.

V *Literary Theories and Criticism*

MacDonald was far from being a "natural-born," unsophisticated author; he generally had a fairly clear idea of what he was doing and why, although his ideas of literary excellence needed modification. Although he had theories about both conventional and symbolic fiction and applied them in his own works, it should not be assumed that MacDonald was a brilliant or profound critic. Before we consider his creative works we should note his scattered, incomplete, but often shrewd critical insights; but we must then examine his fiction in the light of more rigorous modern standards.

MacDonald's deliberate didacticism is perhaps the most significant of his fictional precepts. Ronald MacDonald, his second son, records the following conversation with his father, for which no date is given:

Once I asked him why he did not, for change and variety, write a story of mere human passion and artistic plot. He replied that he would like to write it. I asked him then further whether his highest literary quality was not in a measure injured by what must to many seem the monotony of his theme—referring to the novels alone. He admitted that this was possible; and went on to tell me that, having begun to do his work as a Congregational minister, and having been driven . . . into giving up that professional pulpit, he was no less impelled than compelled to use unceasingly the new platform whence he had found that his voice could carry so far.[24]

As we may note, the most important single event in MacDonald's life was his loss of his pulpit and his reaction to that loss. Scarcely any other writer of fiction in any literature so consciously regarded his function to be that of a teacher and preacher, rather than to be that of an entertainer, artist, or money-earner.

Several characteristics of MacDonald's conventional novels are presented in his critical writings as part of his didacticism. The classic happy ending, for instance, is presented as the *duty* of a writer who is also a teacher: "Donal had none of the objections of truncated people to the presentation of the right as victorious; they say it is not so in life. I say it is. . . . To teach children that vice may have the best of it, would be to teach them that there is no God. . . . No teacher's object should be to train such as the world counts heroes or successful men, but lovers of the truth. . . . Truth and right are the lords of this world also, and must ultimately prevail." As might be expected, religious content is likewise defended: "Why is it that men and women will welcome any tale of love, devotion, and sacrifice from one to another of themselves, but will turn from the least hint at the existence of a perfect love at the root of it all?" [25] The modern reader cannot help but feel that these two didactic precepts are at the root of Mac-Donald's general inferiority as a realistic novelist.

Other characteristics of MacDonald's fiction are defended with less direct references to didacticism but with a similar consciousness of the objections which critics might raise. The existence of sensational elements in purportedly realistic stories apparently bothered MacDonald's literary conscience considerably: "I had found that invention is ever ready to lose the forms of life. . . . As it is, I doubt much if any of my books are more than partially true to those forms, . . . But I believe I have been true to the heart of man. . . . Hence, although most of my books have seemed true to some, they have all seemed visionary to most."

But, MacDonald continued, "Nowadays, the vulgar notion of what is life-like in any annals is to be realized by sternly excluding everything but the commonplace. . . . But I believe that this is at least quite as unreal a mode of representing life as the other extreme." [26]

Coincidence, that feeblest crutch of the plot-maker, is prominent in MacDonald's stories; but he again defends himself, on the ground that the supposedly improbable is less so than we think: "I do not believe we notice half of the coincidences that float past us on the stream of events. Things which would fill us with astonishment, and probably with foreboding, look us in the face and pass us by, and we know nothing of them." [27] Interestingly enough, MacDonald justifies his own practice in terms of the idea that experience *is* full of coincidences, a "realistic" criterion based simply upon observation of real life, rather than a "theoretical" argument attempting to *explain* the prevalence of coincidence in human experience. MacDonald's fondness for happy endings was explained, however, in terms not of observation but of faith that the right must prevail, despite experience to the contrary. Charles Dickens, by contrast, justified his own frequent use of coincidence on the shakier basis of mantaining that a "Divine Providence" introduces coincidence into our lives against all probability. My inclination is to prefer MacDonald's theorizing to that of Dickens; it is MacDonald who invokes the purely "novelistic" criterion of observation, while Dickens in this case invokes irrelevant metaphysics.

The clear pattern that emerges in the passages just quoted is that MacDonald recognized that his stories were not "lifelike" in the opinion of his actual or potential detractors, but he defended them by disparaging the idea that life is either dull or unjust. Even so, it is obvious that he cared more for "spiritual truth" as he conceived it than for strict credibility. After all, he knew that conditions of the "marketplace" demanded realism of a sort, and he attempted to provide it. But, when we shift our attention to the fantastic, MacDonald speaks with greater conviction and authority. Recognizing the distinction between the realistic and the imaginative, he declined to apologize for his occasional forays into fantasies, although these words probably alienated much of his usual audience: "I am well aware that such tales are not of much account, at present. . . . But, seeing so much of our life must be spent in dreaming, may there not be a still nook . . . where, in the pauses of labor, a man may sit down, and dream such a day-dream as I now offer to your acceptance?" In defending his practice of symbolic narrative, MacDonald occasionally presumed to suggest that Jesus also embodied his ideas in parables. But Mac-Donald was wary of the dangers of mechanical allegory:

> A fairytale is not an allegory. There may be allegory in it, but it is not an allegory. He must be an artist indeed who can, in any mode, produce a strict allegory that is not a weariness to the spirit.
> Indeed, any attempt to teach morals allegorically must lack that vivifying fire of faith working in the poorest representation of a history which the people heartily believed and loved [in the Elizabethan period].[28]

As we shall see, MacDonald's fantasies are not wooden allegory; they are something else—something for which he himself apparently had no name.

In any case, MacDonald considered the invention of fabulous worlds to be not only legitimate enterprise but also, as has been suggested already, a perhaps valid speculation about the afterlife:

> The natural world has its laws, and no man must interfere with them in the way of presentment any more than in the way of use; but they themselves may suggest laws of other kinds, and man may, if he pleases, invent a little world of his own, with its own laws; for there is that in him which delights in calling up new forms— which is the nearest, perhaps, he can come to creation. When such forms are new embodiments of old truths, we call them products of the Imagination; when they are merely inventions, however lovely, I should call them the work of the fancy.[29]

Here, incidentally, MacDonald introduces that favorite vexed critical question of the nineteenth century—the supposed distinction between "fancy" and "imagination." Wordsworth, Coleridge, Leigh Hunt, and Ruskin had agreed that the fancy, however charming its products, is somehow inferior, although they reached different conclusions as to wherein the inferiority lies.[30] MacDonald's position is clear, though not especially helpful: he believes that nonrealistic inventions serve their highest purpose (imagination) only when they are embodiments of Truth. Unfortunately

and inevitably, he fails to find a criterion for distinguishing the
True from the trivial and the conscious from the unconscious, nor
does he present a method whereby we can "correctly" interpret
just what Truth there may be in such an invention.

MacDonald's judgment in neglecting to round out a theory of
imagination is wise: he realizes that the interpretation of symbolism is a subjective thing, one best left to the individual reader:
"Everyone who feels the story, will read its meaning after his own
nature and development: one man will read one meaning into it,
another will read another." Whatever a symbolic story "means,"
even if its didactic purpose is manifest, its implicit content may
not be merely what the author "intended" it to mean. MacDonald
ingeniously accounts for this truism of twentieth-century criticism,
which has termed the idea the avoidance of the "international fallacy": "The fact that there is always more in a work of art—which
is the highest human result of the embodying imagination—than
the producer himself perceived while he produced it, seems to us
a strong reason for attributing to it a larger origin than the man
alone—for saying at the last, that the inspiration of the Almighty
shaped its ends." [31] And in this statement we see again the integra-
tion characteristic of George MacDonald of literary theory with
religious doctrine. If we misunderstand a symbolic author, it may
be, according to MacDonald, that we are not yet sufficiently "en-
lightened" to understand him, not yet having reached that stage in
the stepwise process of our spiritual education at which a particular truth is comprehensible to us.

The final building block in MacDonald's shrewdly incomplete
theory of the didactic function of the imagination involves speculation as to the *modus operandi* of the individual symbol, the indivisible atom of imaginative plot-structure. Here again we must
refer back to his religious and mystical ideas, specifically to the
idea that every natural object has a spiritual meaning. A single
symbol has, in fact, a large number of possible meanings:

A single thing would sometimes seem to be and mean many things,
with an uncertain identity at the heart of them, which kept con-
stantly altering their look. . . . While without a doubt, for instance,
that I was actually regarding a scene of activity, I might be, at the
same moment, in my consciousness aware that I was perusing a
metaphysical argument.

I was trying to find the root of a manifestation, the spiritual truth whence a material vision sprang; or to combine two propositions, both apparently true, either at once or in different remembered moods, and to find the point in which their invisible converging lines would unite in one, revealing a truth higher than either and differing from both, though so far from being opposed to either, that it was that whence each derived its life and power.[32]

VI *Theory versus Practice*

As a philosopher—religious, psychological, social, and literary —MacDonald is an interesting thinker who should not be forgotten. But his significance and value as a writer depend finally upon the success with which he dramatizes these ideas in fiction. Many philosophers fail as novelists, and many novelists only succeed in making fools of themselves as abstract thinkers when they try to explain what they are doing. George MacDonald's claim to significance as *both* an artist and a thinker rests upon the success with which his ideas are suitably given artistic formulation in his fantastic works and less suitably in his conventional novels. The next two chapters examine his successes in fantasies and his relative failures in his novels.

CHAPTER 3

The Realistic Fiction

THE first two chapters have suggested many of the general characteristics of MacDonald's "realistic" fiction: it is conventional, proper, optimistic, didactic, sentimental, verbose. Most of these are the very attributes of Victorian fiction which the twentieth century is fondest of deploring; but many people smugly deplore *anything* "Victorian," often without knowing what they are talking about. Properly used, the term is an accurate, descriptive, objective one, to designate the essence of a historical period which, like every other, is both ridiculous and exciting, monstrous and tender, base and sublime—each in its own peculiar way.

George MacDonald's twenty-nine realistic novels may be treated collectively, in order to see what is typical of all of them, because they are very much alike—surprisingly so for a body of work so large and written over a period of thirty-four years, from 1863 to 1897. Because I shall treat the novels collectively rather than individually, no plot summaries of individual works will be presented, except for one: I consider *Alec Forbes of Howglen* MacDonald's best novel and shall summarize it at some length. For the rest, they are so alike, and almost all are as plots so intricate and banal, that it should prove more helpful to know what the characteristics of some hypothetical "typical" MacDonald novel are.

Two paramount conditions obviously account for many of MacDonald's habits as a novelist: he wrote for a living, and he wanted to spread his essentially religious message to as many readers as possible. From these two causes, together with the literary taste of the average Victorian reader, follow most of the superficial characteristics of MacDonald's conventional fiction. From this conventionality, in turn, follow other general attributes. The plots are based on a few formulas; the characters are usually stereotypes;

the thematic issues are derivative; and the mechanisms of suspense and motivation are sensational and artificial. MacDonald was too busy to be a deliberate craftsman, nor did his popular audience demand craftsmanship of him. Yet among his stories there is plenty of excellent material—authentic dialogue, shrewd characterization, and lively drama. He displays the virtues as well as the faults of his era.

But before discussing MacDonald's plots, characters, and settings in his realistic fiction, I must say something about another aspect of his conventional work: his style. Here he cannot be "excused" in terms of his having been simply typical of his era, for he was not. Two biographical factors, peculiar to MacDonald and not especially representative of the Victorian novelist as a type, act in MacDonald's novels to make them decidedly unpalatable to the twentieth-century cosmopolitan reader of English literature. First of all, of course, MacDonald's dialogue is often in lowland Scots dialect, which few now understand, especially in the United States. Secondly, MacDonald's experience as a minister before he became a novelist rather infected his prose with pulpit, as distinguished from fictional, stylistic traditions.

I *Style*

Prose style in conventional realistic fiction, especially that which is aimed at the widest possible readership, is ordinarily and almost by definition in the vocabulary of the masses. What is called "local color"—that is, typographical representation of accents and vocabulary which is regional—is respectable enough: one has only to think of the vocabulary of William Faulkner's southern regional works, in which for example the word "chap" means "child." Faulkner's reader soon gets used to such "exotic" vocabulary, learning the comparatively few unfamiliar words scattered among the predominantly standard vocabulary. But MacDonald's lowlands vocabulary, especially in his dialogue, is of an entirely different order—perhaps more comparable to reading Chaucer in Middle English than to reading Faulkner. To many, the language of MacDonald's characters will so closely approach unintelligibility that the ordinary reader will simply abandon the attempt to read him. Here is a typical example from *Sir Gibbie* (1879), one of his Scots dialect novels (I, 11):

"Wha's that ye're colloguin' wi', Mysie?" asked her mother, somewhat severely, but without lifting her eyes from her *wires*. "Ye maunna be speykin' to loons i' the street."

"It's only wee Gibbie, mither," answered the girl in a tone of confidence.

"Ou weel!" returned the mother, "he's no like the lave o' loons."

"But what had ye to say till him?" she resumed, as if afraid her leniency might be taken advantage of. "He's no fit company for the likes o' you, 'at his a father an' mither, an' a chop (*shop*). Ye maun hae little to say to sic rintheroot laddies."

Several words from this passage present no great problem because of context and their resemblance to standard English forms: *maunna* means "mustn't," *Ou weel* means "Oh well," *till* means "to," and *sic* means "such." Others can be figured out with a little ingenuity: *colloguin'* presumably means "having a colloquy," and *lave* means "rest" (we may so conclude by analogy to the verb "leave"—that is, *lave* is that which is left, the rest, the others). It is a temptation to think that *loons* means "lunatics," but it does not: it means "boys," with no pejorative connotation. The term is so common in MacDonald that we soon pick it up by a sort of osmosis, as we easily do with such common Chaucerian words as *swink*, which means "work." MacDonald himself italicizes *wires* without telling us what it means, but in the scene in question Mysie's mother is knitting, so we can make the correct guess that the term means "knitting-needles." In the case of *chop*, MacDonald's parentheses let us know that its spelling indicates a regional pronunciation of a standard word rather than an item of dialect vocabulary. But what are we to say of *rintheroot?* It is rare enough so that we cannot acquire it as we do *loons*, simply by repetition. Although I have read all of MacDonald's works, I can only guess from context that this one must mean something like "poor" or "lower-class."

In reading a novel, however, one wants to move through the pages with some rapidity; it is frustrating to have to stop and "decode" passages such as this one, and if one skips over them there is the uneasy feeling that something important may have been missed. Further, there is the knowledge that MacDonald is no giant of literature like Chaucer or Faulkner, from whom we expect a due reward for our efforts. And, finally, there is the very *density* of strange vocabulary in such passages. Together, these factors add up to a difficulty which can be most discouraging.

Even more repellent to the modern reader is MacDonald's pulpit style. MacDonald evidently carried over from his experience as a preacher the outmoded nineteenth-century tradition dictating that especially solemn discourse requires tortured, unnatural, and pompously archaic expression. The scenes between lovers are particularly painful: the hero falls into a quite incredible mode of discourse involving expressions like "thou dost not" when his normal phrase would have been "you don't." Thackeray, for example, would never make such a mistake. A few other oddities of expression in solemn scenes may be mentioned. From the language both of the pulpit and of bad poetry MacDonald habitually takes such words as "ere" (meaning "before") and "o'er" ("over"), in the mistaken impression that they lend dignity to speech and description. Besides the pulpit and already-outmoded poetic practice as sources of unnatural pomposity in style, a third might be mentioned: MacDonald apparently became excessively conscious of so-called good grammar when anxious to impart elevation to his language. An example is his use of the word "withal" to end a sentence in which a less self-conscious writer would have used "with." The word "withal" does *not* mean "with": it means "moreover" or "nevertheless" and is archaic even so, though in Middle English and Shakespeare it was used for "with" at the end of sentences. I suppose that, as a man who spoke Scots dialect in his youth, MacDonald may have been overconscious of what he thought to be grammatical propriety in British English and feared that to end a sentence with a preposition would be a solecism; the precept is an invention of the schoolmarm ignorant of genuinely "correct" grammar, or of the pedant.

In any case, the effect of MacDonald's "elevated" style is of pomposity and unnaturalness, of straining for effect, of false eloquence. This is not to say that he *always* writes this way in his novels, for often his language is easy and fluent, and sometimes it is powerful; but that makes the lapses all the more glaring and dissonant. (It is worth observing that artificiality of language is *not* out of place in *non*realistic fiction, where the exotic is native.)

II *Plot*

The plotting of MacDonald's novels has one characteristic common to all of them: the conventional happy ending. As we have

seen, MacDonald's optimism evidently demanded it, although the
logic which dictates that God must reward virtue in *this* world is
obscure and even absurd by orthodox Christian standards. (That
is, suffering on earth is unfair but will be rewarded in heaven;
MacDonald rejected this idea.) Occasionally, MacDonald even
resorts to a *deus ex machina* of the most improbable and "unrealistic" sort. In *Wilfrid Cumbermede* (1872), for instance, the protagonist learns after much detective-work that he is the legal heir
to a large estate instead of being merely the scion of an inferior
branch of the family. However, his beloved has already married
the usurping cousin who is, of course, a rather nasty fellow.
Nobly, Wilfrid decides not to claim his heritage because it would
deprive the girl of the comfort of this cad's luxurious household.
The final chapter begins with a soliloquy in which Wilfrid, the
narrator, accepts his misfortune as the will of God: "Whatever has
been his will is well—grandly well—well even for that in me
which feared, and in those very respects which it feared might not
be well. The whole being of me past and present shall say: it is
infinitely well, and I would not have it otherwise. . . . Yes—
final submission of my will to the All-will—I would meet it *knowing what was coming*." [1]

Thus far the story, one of MacDonald's very best, has led to an
exemplary affirmation of a cardinal moral tenet: that we must accept our fate even if unfair. It is believable, logical, admirably
executed. But MacDonald could not resist; he largely destroys the
effect in the last three pages, just for the sake of a happy ending at
the expense of moral point. The cousin dies young for no good
reason other than that the ending must be happy; the young
widow is to be evicted in favor of a distant male branch of the
family; the hero hesitates and ponders pressing his claim in order
to turn the mansion over to her. While he thinks it over, the girl
summons him, and we gather that he will take over widow and
estate together. Virtue is rewarded—but a nice point is marred in
the process.

Almost the same thing happens in *Annals of a Quiet Neighborhood* (1867). This time the hero is a young minister who courts
the daughter of his richest parishioner, but he cannot obtain the
mother's consent to their marriage. The mother instead tries to
force the girl to wed a duly villainous, hypocritical, and wealthy
landlord. Bravely, the minister decides that it would be ignoble to

expose the villain's baseness by making public the damning facts about one of his "Evil Deeds" of which the parson has learned in confidence. Such a real problem should not be solved too easily; but with an unlikely twist of the plot, MacDonald has the boy get the girl; for self-sacrifice always *pays*. In fact, the reader has the uncomfortable feeling that the author recommends noble selfless-ness not because it is unconditionally good but because, on scarcely selfless grounds, it pays.

The similarities between *Wilfrid Cumbermede* and *Annals of a Quiet Neighborhood* might be multiplied almost indefinitely from the rest of MacDonald's conventional novels. The point is that these parallels are not accidental. Almost all of these works may be reduced to a few plot-formulas: boy-meets-and-marries-girl, young-man-grows-up-and-finds-God, or poor-boy-lives-nobly-and-inherits-title. Such repetition is to be expected from a mass-producing author, of course, but we occasionally wonder how MacDonald held his wide readership when he was so repetitious.

It must be admitted, however, that, despite the general same-ness of MacDonald's plots, the subsidiary issues show consider-able variety. Frequently, he deliberately treats a subject of cur-rent topical interest within one of his trite frameworks. *Paul Faber, Surgeon* (1879), for instance, is an antivivisectionist tract which deals generously with an unmarried mother, features a life-saving blood transfusion, and even treats an atheist scientist with remarkable tolerance—although MacDonald rather spoils the effect by half-converting him. In MacDonald's first novel, *David Elginbrod* (1863), the villain is a sneaky hypnotist reminiscent of Cagliostro, and with an even more sinister name—Herr von Funkelstein. Vivisection, transfusion, and hypnotism were, of course, exciting and imperfectly understood scientific frontiers when MacDonald was writing about them.

Usually, however, the issues are both less topical and less cred-ible. The conflict is between Love and Honor in several of the novels, and these classic ingredients are treated in the tritest imag-inable terms. Almost always, as in *Annals of a Quiet Neighbor-hood*, the hero is *both* honorable and lucky in love, rather sapping the tragic potentialities of the conflict formula. It is interesting to compare in this respect the only two novels in which a noble man *fails* to get the girl—*Sir Gibbie* and *Malcolm* (1875). In *Sir Gib-bie* there are two heroes, the title character and a Burnsian shepherd-poet named Donal Grant, who resigns his claim to the heroine in favor of the saintly Gibbie. In *Malcolm*, Malcolm likewise cannot marry the heroine since, in the process of unraveling his obscure ancestry, he learns that she is his half-sister. It is no accident that these are the only MacDonald novels with sequels: Donal finds a wife in *Donal Grant* (1883), and Malcolm is married at the end of *The Marquis of Lossie* (1877).

Another point about the *Malcolm-Marquis* novels is that, in the former, the hero is a poor fisherman who discovers that he should have inherited a title which has passed to his half-sister, but he refuses to make her miserable; at the end of *Malcolm*, he nobly keeps the information about his right to the title to himself, just as Wilfrid Cumbermede had done. Naturally, he eventually claims the title, out of the purest motives, in the sequel. In order to accomplish this satisfying outcome, MacDonald was forced to change the character of Malcolm's sister drastically: in *Malcolm*, she is angelic; in *The Marquis of Lossie*, she becomes vain and needs for her correction the punishment of losing the title in which she has reveled. MacDonald's insistence upon rewarding self-sacrifice leads in this case to his violating consistency of characterization.

Despite the frequently formulaic nature of his plots, MacDonald's are rarely downright dull. Perhaps, in fact, he could be included in the school of Victorian sensation novelists (a term customarily applied to three of MacDonald's contemporaries: Dickens, Charles Reade, and Wilkie Collins). Several MacDonald novels include a quite fascinating detective-story element, usually involved with the discovery of somebody's mysterious ancestry. MacDonald understood perfectly well the favorite means of achieving suspense: to withhold the crucial information from the reader and to reveal it only gradually to him and to the protagonist.

Another device for the achievement of suspense is the inclusion of apparently supernatural elements in what otherwise seems to be a perfectly realistic story. In the end, of course, what seemed supernatural has a perfectly natural explanation. MacDonald characteristically waits to explain away his spooks until the last chapter, as he does in *David Elginbrod*, where the ghosts turn out to be either somnambulists or hallucinations induced by the sinister hypnotist von Funkelstein. This technique of titillation is, of course, hardly original; among MacDonald's forerunners, Mrs. Radcliffe perfected the rationalization of supernatural appearances in the last chapter to a degree which MacDonald rarely approached.

There is one novel, however, which is built upon a supernatural concept *without* any effort to explain it away. *The Portent* is about a fated couple who are both gifted, or cursed, with the legendary "second sight" of Celtic folklore. MacDonald himself denied having this talent, but his father apparently saw an apparition of another son just after the latter had died and before the old man learned of his death. The incident led MacDonald to accept this uncanny phenomenon rather than to make "rational" explanations for it. In *The Portent*, "second sight" is accepted as a matter-of-fact natural phenomenon and treated in a perfectly realistic manner. It may be mentioned in connection with this novel that in its original magazine serial version the author left the lovers ununited, but the hero-narrator anticipates union with his beloved in the afterlife. When he revised the story, MacDonald invoked the Muse of the Happy Ending to enable them to marry at last.[2]

Sometimes MacDonald organizes his plots around a subject of topical or personal interest, as with the antivivisectionism of *Paul Faber, Surgeon*. Here is one place in which his interest in sexuality is strikingly represented. Dr. Faber learns that, before their marriage, his wife had mothered an illegitimate child—because, of course, of a villainous seducer. The idealistic physician is horrified, and his wife begs to be forgiven. In her agony, she strips herself naked before her husband and begs him to whip her as punishment for her crime. Such sadomasochistic or otherwise violent episodes have led Professor Wolff to conclude that MacDonald himself must have been a repressed sadist.[3]

Wolff's conclusion, however, is at least debatable. It seems more likely, in view of MacDonald's keen awareness of the workings of his own mind, that he was quite consciously catering to the tastes, no doubt depraved enough, of his readers; he had simply discovered sadism as a human phenomenon sufficiently interesting to merit fictional representation (Faber, of course, does not whip his wife). If the fictional representation of cruelty and violence is to be taken as symptomatic of their presence in the psychic makeup of every author in whose works they appear, what artist is immune to the accusation? For that matter, perhaps none of us is immune, in which case the observation is not worth making. Nevertheless, there *are* plenty of violent incidents in MacDonald's novels—enough to convince his readers that the subject fascinated him as it did them. In *Sir Gibbie,* a particularly horrible murder is rendered even more ghastly by the fact that its only witness is a child who is then hunted by the killers.

Perhaps the most characteristic source of excitement in MacDonald's plots is natural disaster: earthquakes, floods, hurricanes, blizzards. *A Rough Shaking* (1890) is based upon an earthquake which MacDonald experienced in Italy in 1887. The blizzard in *Heather and Snow* (1893) is magnificently effective, and there are floods of compelling vividness and terror in half a dozen novels, notably in *Sir Gibbie.* In these scenes, the habitual diffuseness of MacDonald's style gives way to a precision of description, a vigor of expression, as effective as that of any of the masters of English narrative—among whom MacDonald is not ordinarily to be counted. (It is possible to regard his preoccupation with gratuitous natural disasters as an attempt to justify God's ways to man, again in connection with the Lisbon earthquake of 1775, since MacDonald's optimistic insistence upon the necessity of even the most manifestly cruel worldly events here receives its sternest challenge. It is more likely, however, that sheer excitement is reason enough for the inclusion of such events in popular novels.)

There are, finally, a few instances of downright fantasy anomalously interpolated into novels which are realistic in their framework. In *Thomas Wingfold, Curate* (1876), chapters 77 and 78 contain a weird, intriguing story of the Wandering Jew, neatly set off from the novel's prevailing realism by ascribing them to a near-madman. *Adela Cathcart* (1864) is, in a way, a novel only for lack of any better name for such a curious production. Superficially, it is merely another love story in which the heroine is suffering from some obscure malady which is gradually cured by the salutary effect of many interpolated fantasies that are read to her by her mother's houseguests—including, of course, the man with whom she falls in love. This exploration of peculiar psychic states is a persistent plot motif in MacDonald's early works that was later abandoned. Adela Cathcart's illness is largely mental or perhaps spiritual; the heroine of *David Elginbrod* is half-mad from the effects of a hypnotist's machinations; other characters suffer from exotic types of melancholia.

But of the stories in which the exotic and the fantastic provide important plot elements, *Adela Cathcart* is unique. The therapeutic value of the interpolated fantasies is probably MacDonald's way of suggesting to his readers that the fantastic story, generally despised in his time, can be the medium of a healthy Christian therapy more effective than any ordinary novel. The book did not sell, and MacDonald failed in his apparent purpose of reviving an unpopular genre.

MacDonald's plots are often superficial, formulaic, and false, but they are not to be dismissed as utterly worthless. Especially when he was working from his own experience, he could find plenty of opportunities, even in a formula story, for richness of incident and excitement. The reader of the hypothetical typical MacDonald composite novel might be drearily sure that the hero's adherence to the demands of Honor will never leave him hopelessly foiled, no matter what improbabilities may be required to save him, and that, if he is virtuous enough, he will turn out to be the son of an earl. But, on the other hand, the reader will find plenty of original and striking material along the way to the inevitable happy ending.

Indeed, the author of twenty-nine novels may be expected to produce at least one which is better than commonplace; such is MacDonald's *Alec Forbes of Howglen*. In plot especially, this work is intriguing, well motivated, tightly integrated, and more original than most of MacDonald's realistic tales. The two main characters are Annie Anderson and Alec Forbes, whom we meet as schoolchildren in the small Scots town of Glamerton. Annie has been left an orphan at the death of her father, who died possessed of enough money to leave her a very modest estate. This inheritance attracts her father's greedy cousin, a miserly shopkeeper rather amusingly named Robert Bruce and claiming descent from that national hero. Bruce adopts Annie so that, in control of her money, he can invest it at a profit while mistreating her. She is miserable as a student in the school run by Murdoch Malison, a sadistic fellow resembling the schoolmaster M'Choakumchild in Dickens's *Hard Times*, published in 1854 and therefore eleven years before MacDonald's work.

At the school Annie is befriended by Alec, a boy several years older than she, who defends her against the cruelties of Malison and of her "adopted brothers," the sons of the mean Bruce. Alec even fights the schoolmaster when Malison unjustly beats Annie. In frustration, Malison picks on a smaller child, Andrew Truffey, whom he beats so badly that the boy is crippled for life. The incident is the beginning of Malison's reform through remorse.

Annie and Alec are separated when the boy wins a bursary (scholarship) and goes off to a university in a large city. (MacDonald had himself won a bursary and attended the University of Aberdeen; here as elsewhere he makes novelistic use of autobiographical materials.) Left in Glamerton without a defender, Annie is under the thumb of Robert Bruce, but she finds a few friends, notably an old blind woman, the local carpenter, and Alec's mother. At the university, Alec meets an eccentric, whisky-bibbing old librarian named Cupples, who helps him with his studies. Another encounter is with an upper-class, arrogant student named Patrick Beauchamp, who sneers at Alec's rusticity and is knocked down for the affront; thereafter, Beauchamp hates the hero, and at one point he incites a mob of townspeople to chase Alec for participating in dissections at the medical school, hinting to the pious citizens that Alec obtains cadavers by grave-robbing. This, of course, is a topical subject, for medical-school grave-robbers were in MacDonald's day the subject of horror and indignation.

A third important character whom Alec meets at the university is Alec's distant cousin Kate Fraser. She is beautiful, shallow, flighty, self-indulgent, and vain; of course, Alec falls in love with her. Seeing a chance for revenge, Beauchamp turns his charm and class appeal upon Kate, who is all too easily bewitched and, perhaps, seduced, to Alec's agony. During a summer at home, Alec experiences a terrifying flood, compellingly described as usual by MacDonald, during which he rescues Annie. In the book's most moving incident, Malison, who has become a gentler and kinder man, tries to rescue the crippled Andrew Truffey, but he fails and the two drown together.

Back at the university, Kate is abandoned by Beauchamp—there is a hint that she is pregnant—and commits suicide. The despairing Alec now falls into a course of vice, drinking heavily and, it is suggested (but not stated), frequenting local brothels with the more riotous of his classmates. But at this point the odd Mr. Cupples intervenes, pleading with Alec not to fall victim to the alcoholism which has tortured Cupples for forty years. Cupples, in his anxiety and horror at Alec's degeneration, tells the young man of an incident many years before, when Cupples was Alec's age, that led to the older man's drinking. He had catalogued a library in a northern mansion where he fell in love with the owner's daughter, who spurned him; the loss had brought on Cupples's drinking just as Alec's despair at losing Kate had brought on a parallel weakness. The incident is, no doubt, autobiographical to some degree, as Professor Wolff suggests; but we cannot be certain that MacDonald himself had likewise fallen in love, been spurned, and taken to drink and perhaps darker vices. Certainly, however, MacDonald admirably integrates this nearly obsessive theme into his plot.

The pleading of Cupples successfully saves Alec's soul, especially because Cupples is willing to give up his own drinking if Alec promises to do likewise. The agonies of withdrawal which Mr. Cupples goes through are so powerfully and convincingly described that one is tempted to believe that MacDonald himself must at some time have undergone a comparable ordeal; but there is no known biographical evidence for that belief. Reformed, Alec now passes the courses which he had failed during his period of debauchery, and he almost incidentally vanquishes Beauchamp, whom he exposes as a coward and a liar with the aid of Cupples. Now, having finished his medical studies, Forbes goes to sea as a ship's surgeon, in order to earn enough money to pay off a mortgage which the rapacious Robert Bruce has on the farm owned by Alec's mother. The enterprise fails because of a shipwreck; it is Annie who comes to Mrs. Forbes's rescue, abandoning her small property to Bruce in exchange for his discharging the mortgage. Just returned to Glamerton after surviving the shipwreck, Alec discovers that he loves Annie, who has always rather worshiped him; only *after* his declaration of love does Alec learn that Annie had saved the farm at the cost of her small property. They marry, of course, and Cupples, now reformed, gets a better job and becomes a constant family friend. Instead of pursuing a medical career, Alec returns to Glamerton for good and becomes a farmer, reunited with his countryside roots.

There are several aspects of *Alec Forbes of Howglen* which set it apart from and above MacDonald's less effective novels, especially in plot. Every incident is effectively integrated into the story; one never gets the feeling that material is forced into the story for mere excitement, as is often the case in MacDonald's lesser novels. There is even a minor episode involving a visit by Alec and Annie to a local ruined castle—surely an autobiographical reflection of such visits in MacDonald's childhood—but it is worked into the story by having Alec and Annie encounter Beauchamp there in a rather scary scene. At another point, the reformed Murdoch Malison tries to become a minister instead of a schoolteacher, but fails when he forgets his sermon, which he had tried to memorize. This is another favorite MacDonald motif; Wolff suggests that the author in a sense regarded himself as what the Scots called a *stickit minister,* since MacDonald too had failed to hold his pulpit. But the appearance in the story of the motif is far from irrelevant: it serves admirably to engage our sympathy for the changed Malison, preparing for the pathos of the scene in which he dies trying to rescue his own crippled victim. Some of the characters, too, are remarkably effective. Although the self-indulgent Kate, the villainous Beauchamp, and the nasty sons of Robert Bruce are clichés without depth, and although Annie is rather pallidly angelic, Alec himself, Malison, Bruce, and especially Cupples are complex, fascinating persons, clearly not "taken out of stock" but powerfully alive and real.

But perhaps the most striking aspect of *Alec Forbes of Howglen* is the fact that its happy ending is as compromised as life itself. The hero does not, as in so many Victorian novels (including most of MacDonald's own), rise in the world and obtain eventual grace through material and worldly "success"; instead, Alec's reform is rewarded by a good though not brilliant wife, an honorable but humble career as a farmer. One imagines him laboring and sweating, unknown and anonymous, for the rest of his life, rather than becoming a "success" in England as a Harley Street physician and mingling with the nobility as he might have.

III   *Character*

Character, like plot, provides the popular novelist with a rich vein of triteness, and MacDonald never wrote a novel in which he entirely avoided the pitfalls of glib or preposterous characterization. Some of his people become as real to us as Mr. Micawber or Becky Sharp; others are dismayingly wooden, one-dimensional, and unconvincing. The most immediately apparent attribute of MacDonald's clumsiest characterizations is their familiarity. Any veteran novel-reader, especially if he has read much popular Victorian fiction, will groan upon meeting the usual MacDonald Hero—the satirical capitalization is all too fully justified. The Hero is the ultimate paragon, without venality or wrath (except of the righteous sort), full of piety and courage.

One curious attribute of the MacDonald Hero is his impeccable English, considering that he often begins life, as MacDonald himself did, on a Scottish farm. Often the protagonist speaks Scots dialect among his boyhood cronies, but switches to flawless London-Oxford English when he grows up and enters more refined society. In this respect he resembles the conventional Hero of Victorian periodical fiction, as described by Margaret Dalziel: "The boy who by his own efforts rises from the humblest position to one of great wealth and power will speak like an educated person from first to last." [4] Miss Dalziel's study, however, is concerned only with stories printed in the mass-circulation magazines; and she therefore analyzes works of less sophistication than those of MacDonald. But the generalization applies to MacDonald to a considerable degree. The title character of *Malcolm,* for instance, grows to manhood as a fisherman and speaks broad lowland Scots; but when, in *The Marquis of Lossie,* he enters English society, he easily dispenses with his rustic speech in order to woo the upper-class heroine with literate eloquence and piety: " 'My lady!' he repeated, just a little embarrassed, 'I should like to tell you one thing that came to me only lately—came to me when thinking over the hard words you spoke to me that day in the park. But it is something so awful that I dare not speak of it except you will make your heart solemn to hear it.' "

After the pompous sermon which follows, the young lady, apparently forgetting his refined speech (an example of the absent-mindedness of which MacDonald was often guilty), muses to herself: "If what he says be true!—It opens another and higher life.— What a man he is! and so young! . . . He is a gentleman—every inch! Hear him talk!—Scotch, no doubt,—and—well—a *little* long-winded—a bad fault at his age! But see him ride!" [5] In contrast to Malcolm, there is Shargar, the boyhood friend of Robert Falconer. Shargar describes himself throughout as "Robert's dog," and nobody—least of all MacDonald—seems to think that the de-

pendent relationship is not perfectly right. Since Shargar is not
the Hero, but only a faithful retainer, he clings to his rustic
speech.

When we can sum up a fictional character in one word—"paragon," perhaps, or "gentleman"—it is fairly certain that the character in question lacks something essential to the realistic quality of a
novel. Fictional characters should, after all, be approximately
people, and people are too complex to be neatly pinned to the
specimen-board with a word or even a phrase. The MacDonald
Hero is simple—simply a bore; but not all of MacDonald's male
protagonists are Heroes. Many of them experience disastrous
lapses or even begin their careers as moral weaklings before being
straightened out by the uplifting influence of a kindly peasant or
someone of the sort.

To illustrate the distinction between the credible protagonist
and the impossible paragon, we may pair characters whose outward circumstances are comparable. The protagonists of *Alec
Forbes of Howglen* and *Robert Falconer* are two such characters;
both are followed from childhood in a a small Scottish town,
through the University of Aberdeen, and into the world. Alec is a
prankster in his childhood; and, when he arrives in Aberdeen, he
falls into vice. Robert, on the other hand, is merely a saint. He is
incapable of backsliding, even for a moment; and he even seems
immune to the ordinary temptations and lusts which trouble us
sinners. And Robert is also a good deal less credible and human
than Alec Forbes.

Another such contrast exists between the minister-protagonists
of *Annals of a Quiet Neighborhood* and *Thomas Wingfold, Curate.* The Hero of the former is a new minister of preposterous
virtue, while Wingfold at first plagiarizes his sermons until his
conscience is touched by a Cupples-like mentor who recognizes
the source from which one of the sermons is stolen. It is interesting to note, though, that, when Wingfold reappears in several
later novels, he, too, is preposterously and inhumanly saintly.

The pattern of the trite and all-too-familiar Hero is repeated
with many of MacDonald's Villains and Heroines. I have mentioned the sinister hypnotist in *David Elginbrod;* his counterpart
is the lecherous nobleman whose favorite amusement is seducing
the daughters of his humble tenants. The daughters are usually
trusting milkmaids whose "heads are easily turned." Examples of

the Villain are Lord Meikleham, who seduces Lizzie Findley in
Malcolm and refuses to acknowledge their illegitimate child, and
Baron Rothie in *Robert Falconer,* who lures the innocent and gul-
lible Mysie Lindsay to the Continent with a lying promise of marriage and is frustrated only at the last moment by the watchful
Robert. Patrick Beauchamp in *Alec Forbes of Howglen* varies the
pattern by seducing an upper- rather than lower-class girl.

The Heroines, too, are ineffably pure and bloodless; but Mac-
Donald occasionally creates a different sort of girl from the pale,
frail, hypersensitive swooner of too many Victorian novels. In
Mary Marston (1881), for example, he deliberately demonstrates
that a "shopgirl" need not necessarily be vulgar simply because
she is engaged in commercial enterprise. And Kirsty, the heroine
of *Heather and Snow,* is a stout peasant girl, as strong and vigor-
ous as a man. Most of MacDonald's girls, however, are indistin-
guishable from each other and from the supposedly typical Victorian young lady of sensitivity and delicacy.

From these descriptions of some of MacDonald's more banal
characterizations we see that they are all, in fact, the stereotypes
of sentimental literature. The term *stereotype,* to which I shall
refer again, is after all a book reviewer's standby, designating by
definition unoriginality and feebleness of imagination. It is curious
that MacDonald, who was so brilliantly inventive in his fantasies
and sometimes in his novels, should be subject to such censure.
Perhaps the phenomenon can be accounted for by the commercial
necessity under which MacDonald worked, although in a later
chapter I suggest a more complicated explanation. In any case, his
least convincing characters are types; they are members of a group
which may be tagged with a convenient noun or phrase—hypo-
crite, shyster, demagogue, capitalist, or Hero of Socialist Labor.
Bad novels of any time and country are usually likewise full of
type-characters.

But MacDonald frequently presents striking and convincing
people. I have already mentioned one simple departure from the
Hero stereotype: some male protagonists are so eccentric as to be
subject to various weaknesses of the flesh like the rest of us and
are therefore more human and credible, though perhaps less admirable, than the pure Hero. Such departures from oppressive
typicality do not, however, automatically make a character live in
the memory as if he were somebody the reader has met and can-

not forget. Fortunately, MacDonald provides a broad spectrum of people, from the most trite to the most strikingly original and memorable.

One of the immemorial devices of fictional characterization is to base a supposedly invented person upon a real one. Despite the traditional assertion to the effect that "any resemblance between the characters portrayed in this book and any persons living or dead is purely coincidental," the majority of fiction-writers do rely upon resemblances which are not coincidental at all. Such is the case with some of MacDonald's most real people. Greville Mac-Donald's biography of his father points out a number of such cases. The clearest is Robert Falconer's grandmother, a sternly virtuous old Calvinist who burns Robert's violin because it is an instrument of pleasure and, therefore, of the devil. She is patterned directly after MacDonald's own grandmother.[6]

There are likewise several women whose devotion to "visiting the poor" (in a rather patronizing fashion) prevents them from marrying. (Victorian satirists enjoyed suggesting that such females are self-righteous hypocrites who patronize the poor out of a desire to boast about Christian Virtue—like, for instance, Mrs. Pardiggle in Dickens's *Bleak House,* or a couple of nasty remarks in Gilbert and Sullivan's *Ruddigore*—but there actually were many Victorian women whose sympathetic solicitude for the poor was perfectly sincere.) Mary St. Clair in *Robert Falconer* never does marry, but in *The Vicar's Daughter* much of the tension at the end of the story concerns whether or not another such charity-working girl should marry and give up "her poor." Eventually she does. It is interesting to note that the latter girl's name is Marion Clare; evidently, both heroines are named for Saint Clare, the rich girl who took vows of poverty, served the poor for the rest of her life, and founded the order of nuns popularly known as the "Poor Clares." Both of these women are modeled upon MacDonald's friend Octavia Hill.[7]

MacDonald's upright Scottish farmers are pictures of his father; his romantically troubled and skeptical poets are images of his brother Alec, and they die young, as did Alec; no doubt, his religious mystics are self-portraits, executed as diffidently as possible. One especially interesting case of MacDonald's having modeled a fictional character upon a real person occurs in *Wilfrid Cumbermede.* The novel was published in 1872, while MacDonald was still involved in John Ruskin's neurotic love affair with Rose La Touche, and Greville MacDonald suggests obscurely that the story may involve Ruskin's difficulties. Furthermore, as Professor Wolff points out, the early part of the story is filled with both obvious and disguised sexual motifs—one of the several instances where MacDonald dealt with that subject allusively in his fiction. Wolff's *The Golden Key* also contains an elaborate series of conjectures as to the presumed relationship beween Wilfrid Cumbermede and John Ruskin (268–82). It is the most brilliant and perceptive segment of Wolff's study, and the most convincing of his guesses. At one point, the adolescent Wilfrid discovers a vaguely described pendulum machine, and the analysis by Wolff can leave no doubt in the reader's mind that Wilfrid's toying with the object is an allegorical scene of masturbation. Masturbation in youth was one of Ruskin's sources of guilt feelings, as he told MacDonald. In addition, these early chapters involve Wilfrid in a strange relationship with his friend Charles Osborne, which Wolff maintains is homosexual in its implications. Very possibly MacDonald was speculating to himself that repressed homosexuality constituted the basis of Ruskin's troubles, but at this point the issue dissolves into a fog of speculation. We do know, however, from Greville MacDonald's account, that his father was for a time Ruskin's confessor; and, as has been stated, he even went so far as to ask Ruskin whether he was potent.[8] Yet in this case MacDonald's borrowing from life is artistically ineffective, since it is obscured by the "delicate" lack of frankness which he felt was imposed upon him by the squeamishness of his time. We may nevertheless feel sure that MacDonald knew what he was writing about, even if his readers did not.

Finally, there are occasional characters who are likely to be unique in the reader's experience, powerfully original, thoroughly alive and credible, but not simply based upon real people, so far as I have been able to learn. Even among these we find "types," but only in that they appear several times in MacDonald's works without being particularly familiar in Victorian fiction. At least one such person is typically Scottish, rather than typically sentimental or melodramatic—the "stickit minister." It was customary in the early nineteenth century for Scottish Calvinist ministers to memorize their sermons after writing them and then to deliver them as if they were extemporaneous. Occasionally, a beginner

would forget his place and retire in confusion, hurried on his way
by the catcalls of his parishioners. Thereafter, he would leave his
profession and become known as a "stickit" ("failed") minister,
whatever other profession he might fall back on. Such men usually became by default rustic schoolteachers, and carried the op-
probrium of their failure to the grave. MacDonald tells of several
of them, treating them sympathetically and, in *Malcolm* and in
The Marquis of Lossie, making the "stickit minister" one of his
most real and admirable characters.

Another "MacDonald type" is the noble artisan. As I have mentioned, MacDonald followed Ruskin and Morris in treating the
artisan with respect and in emphasizing the dignity of individual
craftsmanship. As a result, he invariably makes his blacksmiths,
masons, and carpenters impressively sound men; *Guild Court*
(1868) contains two such men, a cobbler and a bookbinder. But
the most characteristic and effective of MacDonald's people are
the handicapped saints. Duncan MacPhail in *Malcolm* is a blind
piper who must be almost unique in literature, but is perhaps
derived from the "blind crowder" of Sir Philip Sidney's *Defence of
Poesie.* His highland accent is not MacDonald's own, and is rendered with curious literality: MacPhail pronounces his *b*'s as *p*'s,
and habitually refers to himself in the third-person singular femi-
nine as "she," with confusing effect. This manner of speech may or
may not be authentic "highlandese"; it is very probable that Mac-
Donald got it from Scott's *Rob Roy,* in which novel there is a
character named Dougal who shows precisely the same speech
mannerisms. MacDonald did not know much about the highlands,
but Scott certainly did.

Other handicapped saints are Sir Gibbie in the novel of the
same name, a mute; Stephen Stewart in *Malcolm,* an idiot hunch-
back; and Steenie in *Heather and Snow,* an insane boy who occasionally falls under the impression that he is a collie. In *Guild
Court* there is a weird street-arab girl named Poppie, who is as
odd a literary character as any of Dickens's grotesques. All of
these idiot-savants are spiritual geniuses; they are somehow far
more convincing than any of the paragon-protagonists. MacDonald manifestly believes that children, idiots, and madmen are
somehow closer to God than the rest of us, infected as we are with
worldliness. In his imaginative fiction, too, he gives us a perfect

example of this sort of saint in Little Diamond of *At the Back of the North Wind.*

Such people—kindly artisans, "stickit ministers," and handicapped saints—are something vastly different from the one-sided figures about whom I have complained. It will be noticed that all of them are on the side of Right, even in the case of the misguided Calvinist grandmother of Robert Falconer. As C. S. Lewis remarks, "The 'good' characters are always the best and most convincing. His saints live; his villains are stagey." [9] Although many of the Heroes and Heroines are fully as stagey, Lewis is right about MacDonald's collection of cads, liars, and snobbish old women. Almost without exception, they are never brought to life.

Even in depicting the malevolent souls whom he could not really understand, however, MacDonald was a good creator of a sinister character in at least one instance. In *Malcolm* and *The Marquis of Lossie* there is an evil old midwife named Barbara Catanach who, although perfectly and gratuitously evil, somehow lodges in the memory like an echo of the legendary witches of childhood. Perhaps the reason she is unusual in being a compelling rather than a stagey evil character is that she is *not* based upon a stereotype of realistic-melodramatic fiction like the others; she is in fact a witch, a "type" indigenous to fantastic fiction rather than to bad novels. Barbara Catanach is, indeed, an illustration of the fact that MacDonald's gift, a very great one, is ideally suited to fantasy but disastrously misplaced in the novel—a point already suggested that is discussed in the next chapter.

IV *Setting*

The third member of the serviceable plot-character-setting triad may be said to be a crucial aspect of realistic fiction, since I have already defined that genre as fiction which is set in a world like that in which we live—or at least which *aims* at such veracity of setting. Nevertheless, of course, this world is sufficiently varied to provide the novelist with any number of physical and social backdrops for his drama, and it is his duty to select from the nearly infinite possibilities those which he is especially well equipped to convey most vividly, convincingly, and meaningfully.

The most obvious distinction to be made regarding MacDonald's settings is between Scottish and English places, between the corresponding rustic and genteel societies. MacDonald himself moved from rural Aberdeenshire to an adulthood spent in London, Manchester, Hastings, and Italy. Like many writers, he was most successful in treating the life of his childhood. Again, Lewis conveys admirably the essence of MacDonald's Scottish settings: "All his life he continued to love the rock from which he had been hewn. All that is best in his novels carries us back to that 'kaleyard' world of granite and heather, of bleaching greens beside burns that look as if they flowed not with water but with stout, to the thudding of wooden machinery, the oatcakes, the fresh milk, the pride, the poverty, and the passionate love of hardwon learning." [10] In thus conveying the soul of Scotland, MacDonald sometimes achieves a certain wry aptness of expression in tribute to the severity of the countryside: "The country produced more barley than wheat, more oats than barley, more heather than oats, more boulders than trees, and more snow than anything." [11]

The descriptions of farming, of fishermen at work, and of mountain creeks are usually compelling. If for nothing else, MacDonald has won a place in literary history as the pioneer of the so-called kaleyard school of realistic Scottish fiction, a revival of the nationalistic literature which had been moribund since Scott and Burns. (It is interesting to observe that MacDonald combines Burns's interest in the lowland peasantry with Scott's feudalism in an apparently anomalous but somehow coherent fusion.) The most famous of MacDonald's followers in the "kaleyard school" is J. M. Barrie, with whom it is generally associated; but MacDonald is certainly entitled to be called the school's founder. The movement is characterized by an extreme attention to specific details of Scots peasant life, and it takes its name from the Scotsman's backyard cabbage-patch. Perhaps the earliest such cabbage-patches appear in MacDonald's *Malcolm* (1875).

It was probably in an effort to escape the condescension which usually greets regionalism that MacDonald switched to an English setting with greater frequency as he grew older, but the general effectiveness of setting in the Scottish novels makes the decision seem questionable. By comparison, the English settings, especially in view of the stuffy ladies and gentlemen who usually occupy them, are lifeless and feeble.

But setting is not merely a matter of the country and society in which the story takes place. Viewed in a smaller scale, it is often a question of the buildings and natural scenery which are typical of a given author. MacDonald locates his stories in a few characteristic places, such as the farms of Scotland, the alleys and slums of London and Manchester, and the country houses of the English gentry. Two recurring smaller-scale settings are especially notable: the large, many-roomed castle or mansion, and the underground cave or grotto.

The mansions are often vast and uncharted, with secret passageways, sliding panels, and all the other trappings of the horror story or the Gothic romance. In *Donal Grant,* for instance, the castle contains a huge network of rooms, including a chapel which would undoubtedly be the right place to hold a black mass. The entire complex has been walled up long before the Hero comes on the scene, and it is the main business of the novel for him to find his way into the forgotten catacombs and reveal their secret—which is, of course, suitably dreadful. *Castle Warlock* (1882) contains a similar network of chambers, and so does *Malcolm.* It is likely that this typical setting is a reflection of that experience in the unidentified "house in the north" to which I have already referred.

The two most striking examples of the comparable image of an underground labyrinth of caves occur in *Heather and Snow* and in *Malcolm.* In the former, there is a curious underground barrow, reputedly a relic of the Picts; but the reader gets the impression that it might just as well have been left undiscovered as far as the plot is concerned, since nothing important happens there. The reader feels that MacDonald introduced this favorite setting and then found no functional use for it. In *Malcolm,* on the other hand, many of the most exciting and vivid portions of the very complicated plot depend upon a strange cave set into a seaside cliff, a cave fully equipped with unknown subchambers and cubbyholes. This, too, may refer to some specific experience of the author's, although his biographer makes no particular reference to such a cave in MacDonald's childhood.

If we had only the realistic fiction upon which to work, the persistent occurrence of the related images of labyrinthine castle and network of underground caves would seem mere eccentricities. Fortunately, however, we have a few symbolic works which can be used for comparison, and it should become clear in the next two chapters *why* these two images of setting are sufficiently important in the light of MacDonald's total accomplishment to deserve the emphasis placed upon them here. In the fantasies, as we shall see, such settings reverberate with powerfully suggestive meaning, while in the novels they merely provide the machinery of mystery and suspense.

V *As a Novelist: "Mediocre"*

In this discussion of the elements of style, plot, character, and setting in MacDonald's realistic fiction, I have tried to give a general idea of what the stories are like collectively, without any special attempt (except for *Alec Forbes of Howglen*) to give synopses of nearly thirty similar and perishable works. No amount of summary, however, can quite convey a number of their essential qualities—the verbosity of style, the flavor of the dialogue, the frequent tediousness, the occasional attainment of high excitement and verbal grace. MacDonald's frequently excellent material is invariably mixed with, and usually spoiled by, great flaws. Too often one remembers the long-winded sermonizing, which by any standard is inappropriate to the genre, and forgets the story itself. Even when a place or character sticks in the mind, we are likely to remember with equal vividness the weary turning over of so many, many pages.

Part of this general weakness can no doubt be attributed to MacDonald's desire to please the popular taste, which is nearly always sufficiently debased and corrupting in any century. Even greater damage was probably done to his fiction by the author's deliberate didacticism, an approach that is unsuited to realistic fiction, as is made clear in a later chapter. Even when these perhaps excusable factors are taken into account and allowed for, we agree with C. S. Lewis that there was something about conventional fiction alien to MacDonald, despite the admixture of gifts which *are* appropriate to the novelist. A "born" novelist transcends both his own flaws and the tastes of his generation, as Dickens did. MacDonald was not a born novelist, but we are fortunate in that he did find his appropriate medium in the symbolic fantasy.

CHAPTER 4

The Imaginative Fiction

I *Of Any Length, for Any Age*

COMPARED with his conventional novels, MacDonald's "imaginative fictions" are few, but that deplorable circumstance has its compensating advantages. It means, for instance, that I shall be able to treat these few stories with the fuller attention which they deserve because of their superior merit as literature by presenting a more or less detailed summary of each important work in the corpus of MacDonald's imaginative fiction.

To postulate, moreover, a hypothetical composite or "typical" specimen of MacDonald's fantasies is impossible. Each story has its own peculiarity, its uniqueness, and mere collective treatment would certainly do violence to that singularity. Furthermore, the imaginative corpus naturally separates itself into two general subcategories, since some stories are directed toward children and others toward adults. I have not, on the other hand, grouped them together as "imaginative" merely out of dialectical tidiness, for the same methods and even the same symbols are common to both. The two subcategories differ in tone and subtlety but not essentially in manner or style.

Another way of classifying these works might be in terms of length, since MacDonald wrote both full-length volumes and individual short stories for both his adult and his child readers. The important factor is not what distinctions may be drawn between different kinds of imaginative fiction, but what similarities exist between such artificially distinguished groups of stories. MacDonald's gift of fantasy and symbolism includes and transcends the ages of his readers and their spans of attention.

II *Shorter Works for Children*

From time to time, MacDonald produced short fairy tales for children, mostly to be featured in *Good Words for the Young*, a magazine which he edited for a while early in his professional career. Some of these little stories are rather wooden and trivial in both conception and execution, written as they were under the pressure of printers' deadlines and without waiting for inspiration to strike; but the fact is that most such works are very good indeed of their kind; for, even with a deadline looming over him, MacDonald was capable of astonishing brilliance, charm, and subtlety. Most of these shorter works for children were, in time, collected into anthologies, of which the earliest was entitled *Dealings with the Fairies* (1867).

"The Light Princess," longest and one of the most fascinating of MacDonald's shorter fairy stories, is remarkable both for its humor and for what appears to be, in the humorous context, a rather incongruous sexual motif. In this tale, a princess is deprived at birth by a nasty witch of her "gravity." MacDonald puns on the word by having the princess lose both her weight and the ability to take anything seriously. Her chief pleasure is to swim in a lake nearby, where she seems to have weight of a sort and to be free of the inconvenience of forever floating up to the ceiling unless held down. When a prince falls in love with the princess and joins her in her swims, the witch resolves to spoil the girl's new-found happiness. With the aid of a snake, the witch tunnels beneath the lake and begins to drain its water through a hole in the bottom that has been drilled by the malevolent serpent. Simultaneously, all the springs and rivers of the kingdom stop giving water, all rain ceases, and a drought threatens. Indeed, the drainage of the lake can be stopped only if some man will plug up the hole with his body; and, in the manner of all fairy-tale heroes, the prince volunteers. As the lake begins to refill, it threatens to drown the hero. For a while, the princess cannot take even this martyrdom seriously; but, just as the prince is about to drown, she screams in terror and pulls him from the hole. Her action breaks all of the spells: she regains her weight, she weeps for days, and the springs are restored.

As Robert Lee Wolff remarks, "some psychoanalysts would no doubt have a field day with this story." [1] Sexual symbolism is easy to unearth and impossible to ignore—the phallic snake, the man's plugging the hole with his body, and so forth—but it need not be insisted upon. The Wasteland motif, so familiar to the twentieth-century consciousness since Eliot's poem was written, is also present, with its implicit equation between vegetative and sexual sterility. Here, the drought is identified with the absence of tears, and thus with the child's inability to face the troubles of life with the "gravity" of adulthood.

The entire story is, in fact, a parable of puberty. When the princess has married her prince, MacDonald pictures her looking back nostalgically to her gravityless childhood: "It was a long time before she got reconciled to walking. She had always drifted lightly through the air until that time. But the pain of learning was quite counterbalanced by two things, either of which would have been sufficient consolation. The first was that the Prince himself was her teacher; and the second was that she could tumble into the lake as often as she pleased." [2] Perhaps this reference is to the relative sexual license of the married state, just as the entire story is designed to convince children that sooner or later childhood's frivolity must be abandoned for the sake of mature seriousness, which has its own rewards, as Wordsworth's "Immortality Ode" points out.

"The Light Princess" was one of the interpolated stories in *Adela Cathcart,* and as such was one of MacDonald's earliest attempts at symbolic fiction, although *Phantastes* was even earlier. The symbolism is perhaps rather crude, but the remarkable thing is that it is there at all. It is impossible to doubt that MacDonald was aware of the sexual implications of his story. What he was doing is hardly what we think of as "Victorian," which has become a synonym for prudery. For example, the draining of the lake may be taken as symbolic of the onset of menstruation, a fact which surprises the twentieth-century reader and would have surprised the parents of the subscribers to *Good Words for the Young* even more, had they understood it. (It may be noted, however, that the Victorians were not *always* repressed in their attitudes toward sex, as Steven Marcus points out in his 1966 study *The Other Victorians.* But Marcus is discussing overt and straightforward pornography, not the subtler, symbolic treatment of sexuality found in "The Light Princess.") In any case, the point of the story is the necessity of growing up; the sexual substrata are incidental, as they should be. MacDonald is not concerned with sex for its own sake but rather with its acceptance for the sake of mature adulthood.

As I shall point out, several of the motifs in "The Light

Princess" reappear in several of MacDonald's later fantasies. The equation between the infertile Wasteland and a child's reluctance to grow up into a world of tears crops up again, most notably in *Lilith*, and represents a phase of what I have called in Chapter 2 the "stepwise process of education," a larger and more inclusive subject to which I shall devote considerable attention. Looked at in this way, "The Light Princess" can be seen as a purposefully didactic work, shrewdly calculated to sugarcoat the pill of instruction with apparently ingenuous but actually subtle humor. MacDonald is always teaching, even when his pupils do not notice it, and often the same lesson appears in different guises.

In another remarkable story for children, "The Golden Key," a boy and a girl set out separately on journeys to fairyland, meet on the way, go through a series of odd adventures both together and apart, and at the end are apparently united in the Other World. Mossy, the boy, finds a golden key at the foot of a rainbow and searches through fairyland for the lock which it will fit. Wolff's Freudian orientation leads him to insist that the key is Mossy's phallus, and he concludes that the fairy wise woman of the story is only being practical when she assures Tangle, the heroine, that it is safe to accompany a man who has a key—who is potent. But Wolff adds: "If this were all . . . would we not find the story banal? We must read 'The Golden Key,' however, at other levels: the key may stand for the poetic imagination, for warmth and kindness, for religious faith, for love: any or all of these are talismans which a man may not fully know how to use, but whose mere possession makes it safe for a woman to accompany him." [3]

This observation is Wolff's only one about the multiple levels of meaning continually to be found in MacDonald's symbolic stories: usually, he contents himself with Freudian exegesis, as if MacDonald had nothing else on his mind. It is, of course, useful to be able to spot the sexual symbolism in a fairy story, and no doubt it is surprising to learn that a "Victorian" was sufficiently "unrepressed" to use of such devices. But of much greater importance in literary theory is the very multiplicity of meaning to which Wolff pays only passing attention; for multiplicity and indefiniteness distinguish genuine symbolism from mere allegory, just as hiddenness of meaning, among other things, distinguishes either from straightforward realism. The important point about

"The Golden Key" is not its sexual undertones but its vastness of scope. In it, MacDonald manages to incorporate a great many of the salient ideas which he expresses in his sermons and essays and to utilize nearly every device in the repertoire of symbolic technique.

The tale lacks the coherence of "The Light Princess"; instead, it is what Auden calls a "chain adventure story." [4] From an apparently vast store of invention, MacDonald throws into the story many incidents which are intriguing in themselves but which would not subvert the plot (if it can be called that) if one or the other were omitted, and which are related to each other only by the fact that they happen to the same two characters, Mossy and Tangle. Each such adventure is described in a delicate, evocative, haunting style which contrasts remarkably with that of the pedestrian, conventional novels. The following rather lengthy example indicates the magical and mysterious flavor of MacDonald's symbolic stories. At one point Tangle, the little girl, is led to the cottage of a Wise Old Woman by a sort of fish which swims in the air: "It led her gently along till all at once it swam in at a cottage-door. The child followed still. There was a bright fire in the middle of the floor, upon which stood a pot without a lid, full of water that boiled and bubbled furiously. The air-fish swam straight to the pot and into the boiling water, where it lay quietly." After some preparations are made for a meal, the Old Woman

went to the pot on the fire and took out the fish now nicely cooked. . . .

"But," exclaimed Tangle. And she stared at the fish and could say no more.

"I know what you mean," returned the lady. "You do not like to eat the messenger that brought you home. . . . You saw it go into the pot of itself the moment you entered, did you not? . . . In Fairyland . . . the ambition of the animals is to be eaten by the people; for that is their highest end in that condition. But they are not therefore destroyed. Out of that pot comes something more than the dead fish, you will see." . . .

But the lady took no further notice of it till they had eaten the fish, which Tangle found nicer than any fish she had ever tasted before. . . . And the moment she had swallowed a mouthful of it, a change she could not describe took place in her. . . . By the time she had finished her share, the sounds of all the animals in the forest came crowding through the door to her ears; . . . and they were no longer sounds only; they were speech, and speech that she could understand. . . .

As soon as the fish was eaten, the lady went to the fire and took the lid off the pot. A lovely little creature in human shape, with large white wings, rose out of it, and flew round and round the roof of the cottage. . . . "Now have we done the fish any harm?" she said.

"No," answered Tangle. . . .

"They must wait their time, like you and me too." [5]

Again I must forego any temptation to expound the manifest symbolism of this passage—the fish sacrament, the suggestion of metempsychosis, the concept of death as a necessary step toward a higher existence. It is rather the evocative *flavor* which I am trying to convey, for it is characteristic of all of MacDonald's imaginative works. One observation is, however, worth making about the passage. The reader will have noticed that there *is* a certain amount of preachifying on the part of the Wise Old Woman, who explains to Tangle the meaning of things that might be more effective if unexplained. But, somehow, the lecture is not out of place in this fairy-tale context; after all, Tangle is a child, and she is, furthermore, an alien in a strange world, receiving information about that world's workings in the appropriately humble spirit with which one reads Baedeker when visiting Europe for the first time. By contrast, the sermonizing in any of MacDonald's conventional novels is burdensome and officious; the reader or hearer of the sermon is neither a child nor an alien.

In addition to the two superb stories I have outlined above, MacDonald wrote other short works for children which are of nearly equal brilliance, though perhaps not of equal subtlety and evocativeness. "The Carasoyn" is a delightful trip through a world of toy ships and brownies into which a child is suddenly projected. In "The History of Photogen and Nycteris" the symbolism of light and darkness is developed at some length and with considerable, if somewhat labored, metaphysical subtlety. The hero, Photogen (*phos, genea:* light-bearing), and the heroine, Nycteris (*nyktos, eris:* night-striving), represent the opposites of knowledge and ignorance, respectively. Nycteris is especially well named in that she illustrates the proper attitude of the ignorant: to *strive* amid darkness, in accordance with MacDonald's educational imperative to the effect that in ignorance a person must *do* the little he knows to be right, in confidence that in so doing the next step will become clear.

Others of the short children's stories are similarly suggestive but are less inspired. One of them, "The Giant's Heart," rather repellently involves torturing an evil giant in order to force him to mend his ways; and the story is chiefly distinguished by the dismayingly sticky names of its protagonists, a boy named Buffy-Bob and a girl named Tricksey-Wee. Although most of these works are entertaining enough, none ever reaches the brilliance of "The Light Princess" or "The Golden Key."

III *Full-length Children's Stories*

MacDonald wrote four book-length fairy stories for children, and all but one of them continue to be popular in the twentieth century. Of *The Princess and the Goblin,* which is generally considered the best of these, Auden says that it is "the only English children's book in the same class as the Alice books." [6] This volume contains one of MacDonald's favorite settings, a house with mysterious chambers and corridors; and also has its parallel: a mountain honeycombed with tunnels and subterranean rooms, in which there are two separate networks, one inhabited by human miners, the other by a brood of vicious goblins. The goblins are the enemies of the Princess, and Curdie is a miner's son who rescues her from their plot to destroy her. High up in the palace there lives a wise old fairy godmother (called a fairy grandmother by MacDonald for the sake of variety), in whose room there is a symbolic light which G. K. Chesterton chooses to regard as the light of God,[7] but whose meaning MacDonald carefully refuses to delimit by defining it.

Neither the plot nor the particular incidents can be regarded as very remarkable; but the image of the castle with underground chambers and with a holy force in the attic stays with the reader. The transformation which this typical setting undergoes when the reader passes from the novels to this story for children is astounding: the setting becomes a powerful symbol rather than a mere piece of Gothic claptrap full of spooks and fiends or of hidden family secrets. The Freudian hierarchy of ego (the Princess), superego (the Fairy Grandmother in the attic), and id (the Goblins in the basement) is obvious enough; and their presence reflects MacDonald's independent discovery of these phenomena.

But, when symbolically presented, the triad becomes more compelling and convincing than in either Freud's tomes or in Mac-
Donald's own essay, "A Sketch of Individual Development,"
where the same concepts are presented in straightforward
terms.

Apparently encouraged by the success of *The Princess and the
Goblin,* MacDonald wrote a sequel to it, *The Princess and Curdie.*
In this story the Princess and her friend set out to rescue her
father, who is being slowly poisoned in the capital city of their
country. In the end, there is a grand battle in which the plotters
against the king are defeated. Like most sequels, *The Princess and
Curdie* lacks the power of its predecessor, although its picture of a
corrupt society is penetrating and effective. The work's chief symbolic significance lies in its implicit treatment of political and civic
corruption and in the cellars of the capital which equal the underground labyrinths of other MacDonald books in their sinister
quality.

I have already mentioned in the Preface to this study the rather
anomalous nature of *At the Back of the North Wind,* one of Mac-
Donald's most impressive works for children, and one which I am
in the minority in somewhat preferring even to *The Princess and
the Goblin,* excellent as the latter is. Unlike the other full-length
children's stories, this one has a very real setting, though the
events are not "realistic" in the ordinary sense of the word. The
setting is London sometime during the middle of the nineteenth
century, and the characters are mostly poor people.

Little Diamond, the child-hero, is so very good and innocent
that most worldly folk think him absent-minded or even feeble-
minded. In this respect, he is like some of the saintly children of
the novels, such as Sir Gibbie or the children in *Guild Court.* Little Diamond's parents are a London cab-driver and his wife; his
best friend is Old Diamond, the cab-horse after whom he was
named. Among Diamond's London friends is a little girl who
sweeps crossings for the gentry, and whose earnings are stolen by
her mother to buy gin. (The crossing sweeper is one of the most
outrageous social institutions of the nineteenth century's brutal
perversion of laissez-faire economics and "survival of the fittest":
the sweepers were waifs, usually orphans, cast into the city streets
to earn pittances by sweeping horse-droppings from the paths of
gentry who wanted to cross at street corners without soiling their

precious trouser-cuffs and hems.) The setting in general is comparable to the first part of Charles Kingsley's *Water Babies,* which was published eight years earlier and which may have suggested the idea to MacDonald; but, whereas Kingsley's chimneysweep suffers the cruelties of slaving for the owners of English country houses, Diamond and the little girl undergo the complementary cruelties of the city. As does Kingsley, MacDonald takes his child from a bitter life in this world to another, better existence through the door of ostensible "death."

Perhaps the most remarkable thing about *At the Back of the North Wind* is that MacDonald is trying, in fact, to justify death, that most inscrutable of the ways of God, to children. Diamond falls ill and nearly dies when exposed to the North Wind in winter through a crack near his bed over the stable. His coma is explained as the result of the fact that his spirit is journeying to the "hyperborean regions," an idea taken from Herodotus.[8] The North Wind, personified as a woman who takes Diamond on a sort of guided tour through her domains, is also the force which brings death. At one point, the little boy watches as a storm at sea sinks a ship, drowning all the passengers. North Wind explains why her nature includes such disasters:

"I don't think I am just what you fancy me to be. I have to shape myself various ways to various people. But the heart of me is true. People call me dreadful names, and think they know all about me. Sometimes they call me Bad Fortune, sometimes Evil Chance, sometimes Ruin; and they have another name for me which they think the most dreadful of all."

"What is that?"

"I won't tell you that name. . . . Do you remember having to go through me to get into the country at my back? . . . You were very near knowing what they call me then. Would you be afraid of me if you had to go through me again?"

"No. Why should I? Indeed I should be glad enough, if it was only to get another peep of the country at your back." [9]

Here is another instance of MacDonald's preoccupation with natural disasters and his concern with analyzing and justifying them —a concern also manifested in the conventional novels. It is MacDonald's answer to Voltaire's answer (in *Candide*) to Leibnitz's idea that this is the best of all possible worlds. The natural disasters in the realistic works, however, are never so neatly "rational-ized."

After coming so near death, Diamond recovers temporarily, but he then has a relapse and dies. MacDonald tries to explain to his child readers that death is not an end but a departure to another place which is a good deal more pleasant than the poverty in which Diamond had "lived." Here we have, perhaps, a seminal difference between the children's classics of the nineteenth century and the wishy-washy stories fed to the children in our own time: a hundred years ago a MacDonald *faced* the bitter fact of death and made his readers face it, while the authors of children's stories today seem, with a well-meaning but rather fatuous effort, to avoid subjecting their readers to "traumas"; and they expend their efforts in *denying* the reality of life's grimmer side.

And *At the Back of the North Wind* has a most peculiar attribute of plot, besides its bluntness of implicit content, to distinguish it from most saccharine books for children. Diamond, perhaps uniquely among the child-heroes of fairy tales, comes back again into this world after having had a glimpse of the Other World after death. This oddity is something present in *At the Back of the North Wind* that is absent from the otherwise similar *Water Babies* of Charles Kingsley (in which there is likewise a dual this-world, other-world setting and a blunt facing of death). The idea of trips to the other world sandwiched between returns to this is, as we shall see, typical of MacDonald and of some symbolic significance.

The least known of MacDonald's full-length stories for children, and the only one not still in print, is called *A Double Story*. (This work causes a certain amount of confusion because it appears under a number of titles other than the original one: *The Wise Woman, The Lost Princess,* and *Princess Rosamund*.) Anticipating Mark Twain's *The Prince and the Pauper* (1882), it concerns a spoiled Princess and an almost equally coddled peasant girl who are exchanged for each other through the therapeutic influence of a Wise Woman. Both of the little girls are duly chastened by the experience and eventually resume their original places with gratitude. Although the plot is ingeniously worked out, *A Double Story* is marred by the sort of nonfunctional sermonizing which similarly weakens many of the novels but is usually absent from the imaginative works. For some unfathomable reason, however, C. S. Lewis ranks this story among MacDonald's "great works." [10]

IV *Short Fantasies for Adults*

The brief excerpts from the children's stories should have given the reader an idea of their style and manner; and quotations from the fantasies for adults should also identify these qualities. One of MacDonald's most striking technical accomplishments is that he transferred the fairy-tale technique intact from its more usual dwelling-place in the children's library to the realm of adult symbolic fiction. There are the same fairies, the same dreamlike events, the same evocative prose—but the themes are grave and mature; the motifs, more complex and terrifying. The shorter works are apt to be, as is not the case with the stories for children, somewhat inferior to the full-length tales.

For one thing, MacDonald sometimes chose to write merely Gothic short fantasies, as distinguished from the more largely symbolic and universal concerns which animate the longer ones. In such in-between works as *The Portent, Adela Cathcart,* and at times *David Elginbrod,* MacDonald experimented with the supernatural without endowing it with the suggestiveness and imaginative vividness of his best fantasies. Several of his short tales are of the same sort. "The Cruel Painter," for instance, is a typical Gothic romance, set in Bohemia and dealing with vampirism; but it is entirely without symbolic resonance. "The Grey Wolf," a terror-story in the manner of Poe, deals with a lovely girl who is a werewolf. Like the Celtic second sight which is the subject of *The Portent,* these are traditional subjects of the shallow supernatural tale which is perhaps exciting for a while but which lacks the symbolic force that imbeds *The Princess and the Goblin* in the memory long after its details are forgotten.

Perhaps the best of the shorter fantasies for adults is "The Castle." Like *The Princess and the Goblin,* it is an example of the analogy between a many-chambered building and the mind, complete with deep cellar levels and unexplored chambers. The denizens of the castle turn for advice not to a fairy godmother, but to an elder brother, whose wisdom they foolishly fail to heed. The elder brother is obviously Jesus, but perhaps a little too obviously. The most striking thing about "The Castle" is its starkness of style, which gives it considerable power; in most of his other works, MacDonald exhibits a rather typically Victorian overfloridity of style. (It should perhaps be mentioned that most of MacDonald's shorter fantasies for adults were composed for inclusion in *Adela Cathcart*, where adults are telling stories to one another; after completing this work in 1864, MacDonald rarely returned to the form, perhaps because *Adela Cathcart* was less successful in the marketplace than most of his realistic novels.)

As I have mentioned, *The Portent* is rather a hybrid work, partly realistic (although it contains nonrealistic visions and strange occurrences), in that the apparently supernatural material is rationalized and "explained away." When asked whether the story had any symbolic meaning, MacDonald replied: "You may make of it what you like. If you see anything in it, take it and I am glad you have it; but I wrote it for the tale." [11] *The Portent* is also a hybrid in another sense, in that it is of intermediate length: I have rather arbitrarily grouped it with the shorter fantasies for adults, in part because, like several of the others, and unlike *Phantastes* and *Lilith*, it seems to lack symbolic resonance. The work's chief importance lies in its featuring a library and a house with a network of uncharted corridors and abandoned chambers. Although these settings serve only to provide a rather spooky atmosphere in *The Portent* itself, they are two of MacDonald's obsessions and are endowed elsewhere with profound and complex meanings.

V *Full-length Adult Fantasies*

MacDonald's masterpieces are the two full-length, thoroughly symbolic fantasies for adults, *Phantastes* and *Lilith*. In these books, as in *The Princess and the Goblin, the Princess and Curdie, At the Back of the North Wind*, "The Light Princess," and "The Golden Key," his symbolic techniques reach their fullest realization. And, since MacDonald wrote these two works with adult readers in mind, he includes in them an admixture of terror and evil which he largely omitted from the works for children, presumably for fear of frightening his readers. Both *Phantastes* and *Lilith* are serious, exciting, richly textured, and crammed with astounding imaginative strokes. Because of their excellence, I draw most heavily upon these two works for examples of the typical devices found throughout MacDonald's imaginative fiction.

Yet the two stories are in some respects very unlike each other, as might be expected from the fact that *Phantastes* was published in 1858 and *Lilith* in 1895. *Lilith* is darker and less triumphant, *Phantastes* more in the tradition of the heroic Romance whose hero succeeds in the end. They are even more different in plot: *Phantastes* is looser, less integrated, like "The Golden Key"; *Lilith* is more tightly constructed, like "The Light Princess."

(A) Phantastes. The word "Phantastes" is taken from the name of a character in Phineas Fletcher's early seventeenth-century Spenserian pastiche, *The Purple Island* (1633), but I have been able to discover no particular resemblance between Fletcher's work and MacDonald's. What seems to be significant is that Edmund Spenser and his imitators "founded" the symbolic fantasy for adults, at least in English, although they wrote in verse. MacDonald's *Phantastes* is the earliest such work in English prose, so far as I know. Professor Wolff is no doubt correct, however, in tracing the major influence upon MacDonald, not to Spenser and the Spenserians, but to the German Romantic prose works of such writers as Novalis, Jean Paul Richter, and E. T. A. Hoffmann; Wolff does an admirable job of tracing such influences. The question of the literary ancestry of the genre is of some importance, especially because of the important twentieth-century works in the form by such writers as Franz Kafka, C. S. Lewis, J. R. R. Tolkien, and Mervyn Peake. Lin Carter, who edits the Adult Fantasy Series published by Ballantine Books, argues that William Morris's *The Wood Beyond the World* (1895) is the first English prose fantasy for adults; but there is reason to believe that Carter came to Morris first and learned about MacDonald only later. Primacy, insofar as it is important, clearly belongs to MacDonald's *Phantastes*.

The protagonist and narrator of *Phantastes* is named Anodos, a Greek word usually interpreted as meaning "a way back." Wolff, however, states in *The Golden Key* that it means "pathless" (47); either significance seems to fit the story, in that Anodos is a young man who does not know where he is going, and in that the story indicates his unknown goal as finding "a way back" to the guiltlessness of childhood. I personally suspect that MacDonald had "a way back" in mind, since that phrase occurs a couple of times in the text.

On the day after his twenty-first birthday, Anodos is assigned by his family the bedroom which had belonged to his dead father (his mother is also dead), where he explores his father's old desk. While he is searching for relics, Anodos comes upon a tiny, lovely creature who identifies herself as his "fairy grandmother" a variation upon the traditional "fairy godmother" also used in *The Princess and the Goblin*. When Anodos moves as if to kiss the apparition, she warns him that one may not make love to one's grandmother. Wolff, who cites this passage as evidence of an Oedipal syndrome, points out that MacDonald kept in a secret drawer of his own desk a letter from his mother to his father, expressing sorrow at the infant George's difficulties in being weaned. The psychoanalysis is interesting and even almost convincing, but the Oedipal interpretation is quite irrelevant to the appreciation of *Phantastes* as literature. It may at least be argued that MacDonald was no more of an Oedipus than most of us and that, as in "The Light Princess," he was perfectly aware of what he was doing: dramatizing and symbolizing a universal psychic phenomenon, not because it was unconsciously repressed in himself, but because he knew it to be everywhere.

The "grandmother" informs Anodos that he is about to visit fairyland, and he goes to sleep in apprehension. The next morning he awakens to the second of his adventures:

> I suddenly, as one who wakes to the consciousness that the sea has been moaning about him for hours, or that the storm has been howling around his window all night, became aware of the sound of running water near me; and, looking out of bed, I saw that a large green marble basin, in which I was wont to wash, . . . was overflowing like a spring; and that a stream of clear water was running over the carpet. . . .
>
> My dressing-table was an old-fashioned piece of furniture of black oak, . . . elaborately carved in foliage, of which ivy formed the chief part. The nearer end of this table remained just as it had been, but on the further end a singular change had commenced. I happened to fix my eyes on a little cluster of ivy leaves. The first of these was evidently the work of the carver; the next looked curious; the third was unmistakably ivy; and just beyond it a tendril of clematis had twined itself about the gilt handle of one of my drawers. . . . I thought it high time to get up; and, springing from my bed, my bare feet alighted upon a cool green sward; and although I dressed in all haste, I found myself completing my toilet under the boughs of a great tree.[12]

This passage is an example of what Auden calls "dream-realism." Things do, after all, happen this way in our dreams; the elaborateness of details is characteristic not of dreams themselves, which are vague, but rather of the way we rationalize and make coherent the uncanny changes of a dream when we try to tell someone about it. MacDonald is putting into practice his own critical theory about the invention of other worlds with their own laws, consistent in themselves but quite unlike the laws of this world, and partaking of the nature of that dream world which is our deepest insight into what the afterlife may be like. It may be noted also that the hero's casual, offhand, unastonished *acceptance* of this strange wakening is just the way we react to the odd events of dreams when we are still dreaming; it is not until we awaken that the strangeness of dream-events strikes us as impossible. Auden calls the phenomenon "dream-*realism*" because, as in realistic fiction, the plain "truth" is reported matter-of-factly.

Anodos is now in fairyland, where he undergoes a great many equally dreamlike experiences. What may be called the "shape" of the plot is remarkably unstructured: episodes succeed one another without apparent causal relationship or interconnection (except insofar as they all happen to the same protagonist). The reader feels that the order of Anodos's adventures might often be shuffled without loss of coherence. The protagonist is generally traveling eastward, but a spatial as well as temporal rearrangement of his encounters would not be disturbing; we feel that he is not so much making progress in his spiritual education as simply adding to the *number* of his experiences. Along the way he stops overnight at a succession of houses, huts, cottages, and palaces which he conveniently arrives at just as the sun is setting. Many of these buildings are inhabited by middle-aged and old women who give Anodos advice and explain the nature of fairyland to him; he usually fails to heed or understand what they tell him, and then departs the next morning, none the wiser. *Phantastes* is what Auden calls a "chain adventure story," full of events which are strung out like beads on a string (the string being the central character, who alone connects the episodes) rather than interconnected into a tight network with every event and character connected by causality and relationship to every other. In this, the plot of *Phantastes* resembles what is called the picaresque novel, a Renaissance genre in which the rogue-hero goes from one place to another when a locality "gets too hot for him" because of his pranks and seductions; or it resembles a tale of knight-errantry ("errant" means "wandering"), in which the hero, after each conquest, moves on to whatever adventure awaits him next. Spenser's *The Faerie Queene* and many long sections of Malory's *Morte Darthur* have this kind of plot-structure.

Despite its loose organization, the plot of *Phantastes* does have a certain degree of coherence, provided by several devices. For one thing, it may be read as an allegorical representation of the first twenty-one years of Anodos's life. The story begins just after his twenty-first birthday, and at the end Anodos makes a significant remark upon returning to the real world and to his family: "I had been gone, they told me, twenty-one days. To me it seemed twenty-one years." [13] Presumably, therefore, we are to read *Phantastes* as if each of its episodes corresponds to a childhood or youthful experience of its narrator—but this is not easy to do, since we have little information about the first twenty-one years of Anodos's life to compare with his possibly corresponding adventures in fairyland. Furthermore, as Professor Wolff insists, the story may possibly be read not merely as an analogical biography of Anodos but as an autobiography of MacDonald himself. Wolff's chief suggestion toward this kind of interpretation is the Oedipal motif already mentioned, but I can think of at least one other. At one point, Anodos forms an alliance with two other young men, sons of a local king, who "adopt" Anodos as a third brother. The three enter into a pact to rid the countryside of three giants who have been harassing the kingdom. Each kills a giant in the ensuing battle, but Anodos survives while the other two die as the giants do. This otherwise detached episode is, to anyone who has read the biography of George MacDonald, clearly an allegorical representation of the fact that George and his brothers Alec and John all contracted tuberculosis in their youth, and only George survived it. As always, it is the moral lesson of the adventure that is important, for MacDonald's reader could hardly be expected to know about the family's troubles with consumption. After the battle, Anodos delivers a dungeonful of prisoners who had been captured by the giants and becomes the hero of the hour. But he is uneasy in his triumph: "I was almost ashamed that I was alive, while they, the true-hearted, were no more. . . . I released the prisoners, knights and ladies, all in sad condition from the cruelties and neglects of the giants. It humbled me to see them crowding round me with thanks, when in truth the glorious brothers, lying dead by their lonely tower, were those to whom the thanks belonged." [14] But reading *Phantastes* as an autobiographical allegory throughout would no doubt be unwise. MacDonald frequently expressed his distrust of mere allegory as sterile equation-mongering, and he could hardly have had an emotional experience precisely equivalent to *each* adventure of Anodos. And even if he did, we lack knowledge of the details of MacDonald's childhood which we would have to know in order to establish a one-to-one correspondence; further, it would not be worth doing for the appreciation of *Phantastes,* for the work's merits as literature must extend beyond mere autobiographical allegory. Nevertheless, the allegorical-autobiography aspect of the story does provide a suggestion of unity in a plot otherwise rather incoherent.

Another unifying aspect of the plot lies in the fact that several characters do reappear in different episodes, although most are met only once. The two most important of these are Sir Percivale, taken from the late medieval Arthurian Romances, and a young woman whom Anodos awakens into life and falls in love with. Percivale first appears in rusty armor, the stain having been caused by his having been seduced (we gather) by a fairyland inhabitant called the Alder-maiden (she is a tree spirit, and a sinister one, as is the Ash; Oak, Elm, and Beech are benevolent, while Birch is flighty and undependable). Percivale reappears from time to time, rescuing Anodos from danger on several occasions and, in the process of doing noble deeds, gradually gets rid of the rust on his armor. As for the woman, who also is recurrent, she is at first sung into life by Anodos, who finds her statue embedded in a block of alabaster but awakens her as Pygmalion awakened Galatea. Anodos falls in love with this girl and meets her several times; but she eventually becomes Percivale's wife, and Anodos admits that she has mated with the better man. Other than these two characters and Anodos himself, almost none of the people whom Anodos meets in fairyland reappear after the episode in which they are first encountered. Still, the presence in the story of Percivale and the alabaster maiden *does* serve, to some extent, to unify the story.

A third unifying factor is a rather frightening being called the Shadow. When visiting one of the many cottages inhabited by old women, Anodos is warned not to open the door of a mysterious-looking closet, but he neglects the warning. At once the Shadow engulfs him, and thereafter becomes a constant, sinister companion, blackening his view of the world. In *The Golden Key* (65–68), Robert Lee Wolff equates it with the Doppelgänger of German folklore and traces several parallels in German Romantic literature. Whatever its origin, the Shadow becomes a symbol of great and sometimes rather confusing complexity, as it seems to acquire different meanings in different contexts. The manner of its acquisition, for instance, suggests that the Shadow represents stubborn willfulness, in that Anodos fails to heed the old woman's wise advice. But the first two incidents in which it affects the story suggest a quite different meaning. Anodos meets a little boy whom he regards as quite lovely and who is carrying two magical instruments used by poets (although their significance is not made explicit, I daresay that MacDonald meant them to represent Fancy and Imagination). But when the Shadow falls on the child, he is transformed into a commonplace urchin carrying nothing more remarkable than a kaleidoscope and a telescope. The second incident is similar: Anodos meets a little girl carrying a shimmering and wondrous sphere, but when the Shadow touches it the sphere shatters, to the girl's dismay. This second incident has sexual implications, suggesting loss of virginity and of childhood innocence. Anodos is at first horrified at what his companion does to things that had appeared lovely, but eventually he feels a perverse satisfaction in being "realistic" enough not to see beauty where it is not, in seeing things "as they really are," even as ugly. As Wolff remarks (67), this aspect of the Shadow represents not willfulness but "pessimistic and cynical disillusionment, the worldly wiseness that destroys beauty, childish and naïve pleasures, the delights of friendship and love; it is the foe of innocence, of openness, of optimism, of the imagination." Wolff suggests that the Shadow's acquisition by Anodos has been caused, not by neglecting the old woman's warning, but by his having been seduced by the Alder-maiden—the same way that Percivale acquired the rust on his armor. The seduction incident, if it is that, is strikingly similar to what happens in Keats's "La Belle Dame Sans Merci." Wolff's sexual interpretation seems quite feasible in connecting the loss of virginity with the acquisition of a sour and cynical outlook.

But in still other incidents, the meaning of the Shadow seems to change. After the deaths of the two brothers in the battle with the giants, Anodos feels guilty at having survived; and the Shadow immediately gets blacker because he should *not* feel such guilt. Later, his mood changes to pride in having killed his own giant and rescued the prisoners; now the Shadow fades and almost disappears, suggesting that pride rather than guilt is the "correct" feeling. At other points in the story, the Shadow blackens when Anodos feels smug pride which is, unlike that which he felt regarding having killed his giant, *not* justified, but mere vanity. At the very end of *Phantastes,* Anodos finally succeeds in getting rid of the Shadow because he has heroically sacrificed himself in killing a vicious wolf at a pagan initiation rite which had impressed Percivale but whose evil Anodos had seen. But at an earlier incident, Anodos had met a fierce knight which looked like himself (the Doppelgänger motif again) and had shrunk from doing combat with this representative of his own darker side: the Shadow had immediately grown blacker. Taken together, these incidents suggest that the Shadow represents the guilt which comes from not doing one's duty, and it reminds us of MacDonald's precept to the effect that doing the duty that lies nearest us, rather than avoiding it, is the path to wisdom. In this context, then, the Shadow seems to be connected with cowardice and its removal with courage in action. The suggestion is parallel to the way Percivale loses the rustiness of his armor—by doing righteous deeds. Thus, although its symbolic meanings are multifold, there is a subtle unity among the significances of the Shadow; it comes to represent the complex relationships between guilt and innocence, humility and pride, courage and cowardice, living life and fleeing from it. Yet, since it is really a part of Anodos's self, the Shadow imparts only a minor unity to *Phantastes,* complementary to that provided by the fact that all the adventures happen to the same central character.

The loose, episodic plot of *Phantastes,* then, is not really tied together very well by the reappearance of characters like Percivale and the alabaster maiden, or of the symbolic Shadow. In many episodes, MacDonald appears to "forget" these unifying factors—even the Shadow—and seems to have included some incidents for the sake of mere excitement. I have mentioned several adventures which have considerable suggestiveness, imaginativeness, and symbolic resonance; but I have not mentioned many others which lack these qualities. The looseness and unevenness of *Phantastes* must be counted as defects, though in most respects the work is surely an excellent one.

(B) LILITH. As *Phantastes* is the story of a young man, so *Lilith* is the old man's reemphasis of the same teachings found in the earlier work, colored more darkly now with the repeated disappointments and sufferings of MacDonald's long life. *Lilith* was published in 1895, but it was originally written five years earlier under peculiar circumstances. Greville MacDonald describes the writing of the first draft:

> He was possessed by a feeling . . . that it was a mandate direct from God, for which he himself was to find form and clothing; and he set about its transcription in tranquility. Its first writing is unlike anything else he ever did. It runs from page to page, with few breaks into paragraphs, with little punctuation, with scarcely a word altered. . . . He rewrote it, allowing the typewriter its help, but adding his usual and profuse pen-emendations. . . . Five years intervened between the initial writing and the final book; but in both the same note of present sadness echoes throughout.[15]

In his introduction to the 1925 edition of *Lilith,* Greville Mac-Donald compares the two versions: "*Lilith* was first written in 1890. . . . It had then but a third of its subsequent length; it was simpler in its symbolism, and certain of its points, some thin, were more convincing because less elaborate. . . . The original is of such beauty that it seems to some who have read it that it should be preserved." [16] The entire manuscript (or rather typescript), which has survived and is now in the British Museum (Add. MS. 46187A-H), is an intriguing document. Besides the quite different original version, there are four complete drafts of the final work, each densely corrected, though often with no discernible improvement. Obviously, the author cared very much about the work; and I am inclined to believe Greville MacDonald's assertion that his father felt it to be divinely inspired and took his responsibility most seriously. Of the other MacDonald manuscripts I have examined, none even approaches the complexity and the evidence of long labor obvious upon even a brief glance at this one. MacDonald knew that he was making his definitive statement, not merely grinding out another nearly negligible addition to the immense corpus of his work. For that reason, I shall relate the story of *Lilith* in considerable detail, so that its complex but tightly integrated plot will be fully graspable.

At the beginning, we meet the narrator, Mr. Vane (suggesting both *vain* and *weathervane,* something easily blown about), a wealthy young man who has just graduated from Oxford and lives in a mansion with several servants but no wife. He does not work, but spends much of his time in the mansion's ancient library, accumulated by his ancestors ever since before the invention of printing. Mr. Vane experiences what he thinks are hallucinations of seeing a small man, dressed in black, in the library; he learns from his butler that the house is allegedly haunted by the ghost of an ancestor's librarian, named Mr. Raven. One day Mr. Vane sees the ghost and decides to follow it. Mr. Raven leads him to the house's attic, where there is an ancient mirror. As he gazes at the mirror, Mr. Vane sees its reflections dissolve into a green landscape, and then he stumbles and falls right through the mirror into some sort of Other World (the means of transition between worlds is, of course, very like Alice's in *Through the Looking-Glass*). In this strange world, Mr. Vane meets a raven which talks, though mostly in cryptic language, about the nature of that world—but then, suddenly, Mr. Vane finds himself back in the attic. This has been the first of his several trips into the Other World; *Lilith* shares with *At the Back of the North Wind* a succession of transitions between worlds.

The next day, Mr. Vane sees a raven on his lawn during a thunderstorm and suspects that it is the librarian-ghost in another form, so he goes outdoors in the rain to follow the bird. In the garden, the raven speaks, and Mr. Vane is unexpectedly in fairyland again, this time without the device of the mirror. The raven turns into the old man dressed in black and invites the narrator to visit his house. There, he asserts that in fairyland he is not a librarian but the sexton of a cemetery, suggesting that graveyards and libraries are alike in being repositories of souls. Mr. Raven conducts Mr. Vane on a tour through what turns out to be not a graveyard but a sort of mausoleum, where the bodies of his charges are not shut up in coffins but are sleeping, uncorrupted, in rows. One sleeper is a lovely woman with a dark spot on her open palm (this is the first appearance of the character who is later known as Lilith). The sexton suggests that Mr. Vane should voluntarily "sleep" like the others, but Vane is terrified and runs away, finding himself once again back in his own library.

Now Mr. Vane finds in the library an old manuscript which turns out to have been written by his dead father (Mr. Vane's parents are both dead). It tells of the father's having met the librarian's ghost and having been invited to step through the mirror in the attic; but the father had panicked and had fled downstairs. Mr. Vane then decides that he must not shun the adventure as his father had, so he goes up to the attic, finds the mirror, and again steps through it into the Other World. Sure enough, he again finds Mr. Raven and again visits his cottage, where he meets the sexton's wife; but he is still afraid to "sleep the sleep" and asks if there is an alternative way to learn what he knows he must learn in this strange world. Mr. Raven says that there is indeed an alternative but that it is a long one: Mr. Vane must set off on a journey to—somewhere.

Going westward, Vane first comes to a frightening place called the Bad Burrow, full of terrifying hallucinatory creatures which frighten but do not harm him. Next, he passes into a desert country and travels along a dry riverbed, although he can hear water flowing underground. Thence he comes to a place called the Evil Wood, where he witnesses a fight between skeletons (skeletons, or skull-headed people otherwise fleshed, are a recurring motif in *Lilith*). Emerging from the Evil Wood, Mr. Vane again finds himself in a desert country, where he meets a band of children called simply the Little Ones.

These children are a curious tribe. One of their peculiar attributes is that they never weep and, in fact, cannot, as is the case with the Light Princess; their incapacity is somehow connected with the fact that the area where they live is a waterless desert. The Little Ones are led by a girl, the oldest, named Lona. She tells Mr. Vane of the tribe's fear of two apparently sinister forces which haunt the region's outskirts: one is a race of "Giants" (that is, adults), and the other is a creature called the Cat-Woman by the children. The children sometimes talk a rather gooey babytalk which Victorians apparently found "cute," but which twentieth-century antisentimentalists find, in Auden's words, "shy-making." Sensing that there is something incomplete in the children's lives, Mr. Vane resolves to find out how to help them; he learns from Lona that perhaps a clue can be found in a mysterious city called

Bulika (perhaps *bull* plus *ikon,* a pagan idol, suggesting something like Babylon).

Mr. Vane departs, searching for Bulika but not knowing how to get there. Almost immediately, he falls into the hands of the Bad Giants (called "Bags" by the children), but he is rescued by the children. Next he meets in his wanderings a sad-faced woman who invites him to her cottage in the forest—apparently the same Evil Wood where he had already been so frightened—and identifies herself as Mara (her name is taken from the Book of Ruth, 1: 20: "And she said unto them, Call me not Naomi, call me Mara [Hebrew: *bitterness*], for the Almighty has dealt very bitterly with me"). It appears that Mara is the Cat-Woman whom the children fear, but Mr. Vane finds her kind and she says that she is misunderstood; the situation is reminiscent of North Wind, whom people fear because she is also Death, but who is revealed as in fact a merciful release and a transition to further life, so that such fears are mistaken. Mara has as a pet an all-white, pantherlike big cat, which she dispatches toward Bulika on some sort of message-carrying errand. The white panther's name is given as Astarte, the name of a pagan goddess associated with sex and fertility: the identification is brief, and nothing is made of it in the rest of the story.

After a night spent in Mara's cottage, Mr. Vane once again sets out for Bulika, going in the direction toward which the white panther had departed on Mara's errand. Once again, he finds himself in the Evil Wood, where he comes upon an apparently empty palace which turns out to be inhabited by ghostly people who, although otherwise normal-looking, are skulls from the neck up, Another inhabitant of this palace is a woman who has a dark spot on her side (she turns out to be the same Lilith who, in the sexton's mausoleum, was sleeping and had a spot in the palm of her hand). Uninjured by these skull-people, Mr. Vane proceeds on his wanderings and comes upon a pair of skeletons who are apparently the ghosts of an eighteenth-century rake and his wife, now reduced to reliance upon each other in this afterlife, though they had never helped each other out on earth: they have to hold each other up and patch each other's joints together when, as occasionally happens, their bones start to fall apart. Mr. Raven mysteriously appears and explains that the Lord and Lady are dead souls who are obliged in this Other World to suffer and somehow grow into the fully human beings that they never were in earthly life; they have a new chance, but it will be painful.

Mr. Vane's next adventure is encountering the body of an apparently dead woman, whom he tries to revive. He touches her and feels a very slight warmth, so that he hopes that she is only in a coma; he finds a warm river and decides to bathe the woman's body in it, hoping thus to revive her. The treatment requires weeks, but the woman seems to be recovering. One morning, Mr. Vane awakens to find a wound on the back of his hand, apparently caused by a bloodsucking leech. The experience occurs repeatedly, and he becomes weakened; but finally the woman regains consciousness and tells him that she had seen the leech and killed it. This is *Lilith*'s first instance of vampirism, which (like cats and spots and skeletons) becomes a recurrent motif in the story.

But the woman is, to Mr. Vane's surprise, angry at him rather than grateful because he revived her. She strikes him, and he faints (yet another recurrent motif); awakening, he sees her in the distance and follows her, sleeping next to her that night. In what he thinks to be a dream, she kisses him, and in the morning he has another wound like those inflicted by the leech. In the distance, he sees the woman turn into a spotted leopard, which he follows; when he catches up to the leopard, it is fighting with the all-white panther which is Mara's agent, Astarte. The two big cats have been fighting over a baby which the spotted one has seized and the white one rescues; then the white panther chases the spotted leopard (MacDonald uses the word "leopardess"), and Mr. Vane follows both. He meets a woman who says that it was her own baby who was attacked, and that she had injured the beast, which left a trail of blood. The spotted cat, in fact, is now called an enemy of all children, though for reasons not yet known. Following the trail of blood from the wounded leopard, Vane at last is led to the sinister city of Bulika.

Here, Mr. Vane is taken in for the night by a mother, who tells him about the spotted leopard and says that it hates all children and also that it is a pet of the city's Princess. The next day, he goes to the castle and meets the Princess, whom he recognizes as the woman whom he had restored to life. She gives him some magical wine, and he sleeps; he awakes to find the Princess (Lilith) assaulting him and sucking his blood. He faints again and in the morning wanders about Bulika, seeing the spotted cat in the company of a frightening being called simply the Shadow: it is a flat, black creature of only two dimensions, without thickness. In his wanderings about the town, he later finds the two cats, spotted and white, fighting; the white one is rescuing a baby seized by the spotted one. Now Mr. Raven appears again and explains that it is the spotted cat, not the all-white one, who is the real enemy of children. Mr. Vane and Mr. Raven wander farther and come upon a blue Persian cat, which turns out to be yet another form of Lilith, and Mr. Raven lectures to the animal, addressing it as Lilith (the first time we learn the Princess/leopard's name, although in her spotted form she has appeared before, at first as the "sleeping" woman in the sexton's cemetery).

At this point, Mr. Raven assumes yet another identity; he is Adam, and Lilith is his first wife, before Eve. MacDonald has here invoked a legend associated with the Kabbala, the Jewish commentaries upon the Old Testament. The Kabbalists apparently were trying to reconcile the two different accounts of the creation of woman in Genesis. In Genesis 1: 27: "So God created man in his own image, in the image of God created he him; male and female created he them." But, according to Genesis 2: 21–22: "And the Lord God caused a deep sleep to fall upon Adam, and he slept; and He took one of his ribs, and closed up the flesh instead thereof: And the rib which the Lord God had taken from man, made He a woman, and brought her unto the man." In order to resolve the apparent contradictions, Jewish folklore postulated the idea that Adam had two different wives. The first, Lilith, was created at the same time as Adam but refused to submit to her husband's authority and left him. Therefore, God gave Adam another wife of his own flesh, Eve, who is duly submissive and to whom Adam's children were born after the Fall. But, since Lilith never ate of the forbidden fruit, she was never subject to death; she became an immortal spirit, the perpetual enemy of the children of Eve. The Jews of Eastern Europe teach their children a prayer which is supposed to protect them from Lilith. During the Middle Ages, Lilith became a demon of folklore, changed from an enemy of children to a woman who appeared to men in their sleep and seduced them.[17]

Thus, Mr. Raven, the bird and librarian, who is also the sexton of the cemetery, acquires yet another identity as Adam; his wife is

Eve, and the Princess of Bulika is Lilith. Here is the explanation of why the Princess attacks children and also of why she sucks men's blood. Heretofore, we have been mystified as to why such strange things happen in the fairyland of *Lilith,* but Adam clears up these mysteries in his lecture to the blue Persian cat and to Mr. Vane.

But the story is not yet over, though the mystery has been at least partially solved for the reader. Once again, Mr. Raven (Adam) invites Mr. Vane to "sleep the sleep," and once again Mr. Vane shrinks from death. Instead, he feels that he must conquer Lilith and Bulika in order to free the children in the desert from whatever haunts and inhibits them. Despite Adam's advice, Mr. Vane gets a splendid horse and rides off in pursuit of the two big cats; but the horse drops dead and leaves Vane alone, back in the desert country, surrounded by pursuing wolves. The two cats reappear and drive off the wolves, but Mr. Vane is captured again by the Bad Giants and is again rescued by the children, who stone the Giants and drive them off forever. Reunited with the children, Mr. Vane resolves to conquer Bulika with their aid and with the aid of a herd of elephants which have been tamed by the children. Bulika is duly conquered, but in the fight Lona is killed by Lilith, who is captured. The band leaves the evil city and brings Lona's body and the captured Lilith to Mara's cottage, where a terrifyingly powerful scene takes place. Mara tortures Lilith in an effort to make her give up her self-willed allegiance to the Shadow:

"I am sorry: you must suffer!"

"But be free!"

Involuntarily I [Vane] turned to the hearth: its fire was still a small moveless glow. But I saw the worm-thing come creeping out, white-hot. . . . Mara stood motionless, as one that waits an event foreknown. The shining thing crawled onto Lilith's bare bony foot. . . . Slowly, very slowly, it crept along her robe until it reached her bosom, where it disappeared among the folds. . . .

At length, on the dry, parchment-like skin, began to appear drops as of the finest dew: in a moment they were as large as seed-pearls, ran together, and began to pour down in streams. . . . The creature had passed in by the center of the black spot in Lilith's side and was piercing through the joints and marrow to the thoughts and intents of the heart. The princess gave one writhing, contorted shudder, and I knew the worm was in her secret chamber.

"She is seeing herself!" said Mara. . . . "She is far away from us, afar in the hell of her self-consciousness. The central fire of the universe is radiating into her the knowledge of good and evil, the knowledge of what she is. . . . No gentler way to help her was left. . . ."

"Will you change your way?" she said at length.

"Why did he make me such?" gasped Lilith.

"You have made yourself what you are. Be of better cheer: he can remake you."

"I will not be remade." [18]

After other tortures, implacable and vivid enough to make us sympathize with Lilith's proud refusal to change and thus, she thinks, surrender her identity, she finally surrenders. The shadow spot migrates to the palm of her hand, which clenches over it. Mara and Mr. Vane accompany Lilith to Adam's house of death in the cemetery, where Eve tries and fails to make the Princess open her hand. She simply cannot and begs for assistance:

"There was a sword I once saw in your husband's hands," she murmured. "I fled when I saw it. I heard him who bore it say that it would divide whatever was not one and indivisible!"

"I have the sword," said Adam. "The angel gave it me when he left the gate."

"Bring it, Adam," pleaded Lilith, "and cut me off this hand that I may sleep."

. . . The sword gleamed once, there was one little gush of blood, and he laid the severed hand in Mara's lap. Lilith had given one moan, and was already fast asleep.[19]

One task remains for Mr. Vane: he must take the severed hand into the desert country where the children had lived, unable to grow up or to weep. There he buries the hand, and at once rain begins to fall, the empty riverbeds flow again, the Wasteland is restored. Again, as in "The Light Princess," the mythic Wasteland is connected with the inability to weep—fertility is dependent upon the sorrow of maturity. It has been man's lot ever since Eve's first sin to eat of the fruit of the knowledge of good and evil and to die at last into a better world.

At the end of *Lilith* there are several chapters of rather diffuse mystical visions. Mr. Vane and the children agree to "sleep the sleep" in Adam's mausoleum, but when he does so Mr. Vane en-

counters not bliss but bad dreams, during one of which he even
thinks himself back in his library—yet another return to this
world. In one dream, he fancies that the dead Lona is his destined
wife. In another, he goes with Adam and Eve on a visit to the
former Wasteland, now flowing with water and fertile, and then to
Bulika, which has become a beautiful city reminiscent of the end
of John Bunyan's *Pilgrim's Progress,* or of the Paradiso portion of
Dante's *Divine Comedy,* which MacDonald quotes. But, at the
very end, Mr. Vane suddenly wakes back in his library, back in
the real world after having learned his lesson. There he waits
hopefully for death, which will restore him to his dream of heaven
and to his bride Lona.

The story of *Lilith* has a number of remarkable characteristics.
The retracing of steps, including repeated visits to the "real
world" and to the world of the children, the Bad Giants, and the
Evil City, gives the plot a remarkable flavor, integrating it tightly.
The Kabbalistic substratum makes it resonant with the echoes of
immemorial legend. The repeated motifs—cats, skeletons, vampirism, water—are likewise resonant and echoing, acquiring added
ominous significance with every recurrence. And perhaps the most
striking attribute of *Lilith* is the fact that, at the end, its narrator
has *not* attained ultimate transcendence; he only knows that there
is such a thing after death, which he awaits patiently. There is no
apotheosis—only an awaiting, a partial arrival at wherever Mr.
Vane is destined to go.

Robert Lee Wolff is offended by this longing for death—which
appears elsewhere in MacDonald—and condemns *Lilith* as a sermon of despair. But it is clear that MacDonald is advocating acceptance of *both* life and death, the latter as the God-given if
bitter way to enlightenment and salvation. His very recognition of
life's bitterness is, as it was for Kierkegaard, the absurd reason for
his leap of faith. The very incompleteness of the ending is consistent with MacDonald's view that enlightenment is never complete in this life, though we may have dreams and fleeting visions
of the better world, as Mr. Vane does. If *Lilith* fails (I do not
think it does), it is not through discouraged pessimism but with
the "failure" of Milton, who, like MacDonald, portrayed willful
pride with such sympathy that he made himself, in Blake's words,
"of the devil's party without knowing it."

VI *Plot, Character, and Setting in the Fantasies*

Many of the characteristics of the fantasies have been made manifest in the course of the summaries; and the remarkable contrasts between the plots, characters, and settings of MacDonald's novels and fantasies are perhaps already obvious, but these should be stressed. Similarly, the identity of purpose found in both genres needs to be pointed out; but, for the present, a brief analysis of the fictional elements in the symbolic tales will suffice.

As I have already suggested, the chief characteristic by which the realistic and the imaginative may be most readily distinguished is their setting. In general, what I have called works of "imaginative fiction" are set in some Other World, one which has "natural laws" different from those of the world in which we pass our waking hours. MacDonald himself explicitly makes the distinction in his essay on "The Fantastic Imagination."

> The natural world has its laws, and no man must interfere with them in the way of presentment any more than in the way of use; but they themselves may suggest laws of other kinds, and man may, if he pleases, invent a little world of his own, with its own laws. . . .
> His world once invented, the highest law that comes next into play is, that there shall be harmony between the laws by which the new world has begun to exist; and in the process of his creation, the inventor must hold by those laws. . . .
> It were no offence to suppose a world in which everything repelled instead of attracted the things around it; it would be wicked to write a tale representing a man it called good as always doing bad things. . . . In physical things a man may invent; in moral things he must obey—and take their laws with him into his invented world as well.[20]

Sometimes MacDonald derives the laws of his invented worlds from fairy-tale tradition—as he does when postulating countries where one may walk on rainbows in "The Golden Key," or where the troubles of the royal family are reflected throughout the realm, as in "The Light Princess," where the cessation of rain coincides with the Princess's rejection of puberty. Most often, however, he finds his natural laws in the world of dreams. As I have suggested, MacDonald thought that dreams may suggest to us something of the nature of the afterlife; therefore, he apparently examined his own dreams carefully and took from them whatever

peculiarities struck him. W. H. Auden remarks that "His greatest
gift is what we might call his dream realism, his exact and profound knowledge of dream causality, dream logic, dream change,
dream morality: when one reads him, the illusion of participating
in a real dream is perfect; one never feels that it is an allegorical
presentation of wakeful conscious processes." [21]

For example, we have the curious fact that persons in dreams
often shift their identities and shapes. In *Lilith,* the librarian is
successively a raven, a sexton, and Adam; and Lilith herself turns
at will into a panther or, in one episode, a blue cat. In *At the Back
of the North Wind* the North Wind is personified as a woman, but
at one point she, too, changes shapes. At first she is riding on
Little Diamond's shoulder:

> She jumped from his shoulder, but when Diamond looked for her
> upon the ground, he could see nothing but a little spider. . . . And
> the spider grew and grew and went faster and faster, till all at once
> . . . it was not a spider but a weasel. . . . And the weasel grew
> . . . till all at once . . . the weasel was not a weasel but a cat. Away
> went the cat. . . . But the next time he came up with the cat, the cat
> was not a cat, but a hunting-leopard. And the hunting-leopard grew
> to a jaguar. . . . And the jaguar grew to a Bengal tiger.[22]

As an example of what he calls "dream logic," Auden cites this
passage from *Phantastes:* "I saw, therefore, that there was no
plan of operation, offering any probability of success, but this: to
allow my mind to be occupied with other thoughts, as I wandered
around the great centre-hall, and so wait until the impulse to
enter one of the others should happen to arise in me just at the
moment when I was close to one of the crimson curtains." [23] By so
doing, Anodos catches an assembly of spirits dancing, although on
every previous attempt they had read his mind and frozen into the
attitudes of sculptures as he burst in upon them. When he casually
accepts the "law" that statues can dance, read minds, and come to
life at will when unobserved, he has no trouble in finding a way to
surprise them; they are aware too late of his entrance.

Although such dream settings are inherently alien to the "real
world" of the novels, MacDonald does make use of many of the
same characteristic physical locales in both his conventional and
his imaginative works. The unexplored castle, the underground
chambers, the devastated countryside—all are recurrent motifs in

both genres. The chief difference lies in the fact that, in the imaginative works, such places are more readily endowed with symbolic meanings, as demonstrated in the next chapter. The settings of MacDonald's imaginative works are, in summary, quite consistently characterized by a few attributes: his worlds are unlike our everyday world, with different natural laws; these resemble the "laws" of dreams; and they include such reiterated symbolic motifs as the Wasteland, the uncharted mansion, the library, the network of underground caves and tunnels.

In plot, there are two kinds of typical structures in MacDonald's imaginative stories. One is the traditionally formulaic: prince rescues princess as in "The Light Princess." Such formulas are derived from the literature of the fairy tale, and their occurrence is only to be expected. The essential point is that formula plots are appropriate in fairy tales but offensively trite in conventional novels, as I have suggested in discussing the boy-meets-girl plots of MacDonald's realistic works; but the reasons for my judgment in favor of formulaic fantasies are explored in the next chapter.

The other typical imaginative plot-structure is the chain adventure-story, in which the Hero journeys to the Other World and there goes through a series of consecutive but otherwise apparently unrelated adventures—the fundamental structure of "The Golden Key," *Phantastes,* and (to a lesser extent) *Lilith.* It is also, of course, the plot structure of any number of other kinds of literature: the stories of Heracles and Don Quixote, of Huckleberry Finn and Odysseus, of Augie March and Sir Launcelot. Here, too, MacDonald's practice works well in fairy tales; but, unlike the case of formulaic plots in conventional novels, it cannot be said that MacDonald wrote conventional works with chain plots. Unlike the formulaic plot, then, perhaps the chain story is not *habitual* in MacDonald but represents his practicing a time-honored tradition in fantasy.

Finally, regarding MacDonald's characterization, how can one defend the fact that in his fantasies the characters fall inevitably into types—princes and princesses, villains and heroines, paragons and victims—while complaining about such typing in the realistic works? The clichés of characterization are quite similar, but they seem appropriate in one case and banal in the other. This question, too, will be discussed in the next chapter.

CHAPTER 5

The Symbolic Muse

I *Particular versus General*

EVERYTHING about George MacDonald's character, life, philosophy, and cast of mind seems, in the glare of hindsight, to have fitted him for the writing of symbolic fantasy and to have predestined him to mediocrity as a realistic novelist. His insistence upon didacticism prompted him to spoil many novels by interpolating into them long sermons—good preaching, perhaps, but bad storytelling. His optimism about God's intentions toward men led him to graft sentimental happy endings onto tales where they do not fit, outraging the reader's knowledge of the world when they teach that virtue must be rewarded in this life, however insuperable the obstacles. (The "error" is rectified in *Lilith*, which is neither incoherent nor excessively optimistic.) The triteness and shallowness of MacDonald's ideas about interpersonal morality and interclass relationships, as described in Chapter 2, made his novels dull; for these are the natural subject-matter of realism, which deals with human forces in a social context.

The subject-matter appropriate to fanstasy, on the other hand, is probably abstract morality in a transcendent context: man's relations with his God and his conscience rather than with his fellow man. Finally, as I demonstrate in this chapter, MacDonald's imagination was of the kind which perceives, not the concrete and particular, but the abstract and general underlying the "merely" physical, existential things of this world. MacDonald consistently argued that God would eventually reward the good and punish the wicked. In realistic fiction, whose setting is confined to life in this world, he felt obliged to convey the idea through the conventional "happy ending." As in *Wilfrid Cumbermede*, a conventional novel embodying this idea often displays a last-page invocation of a *deus ex machina* to destroy the villain and join the hero to the heroine. The fortuitous and gratuitous implausibility of such a novel's ending goes against the rule of plausibility which is a canon of realistic fiction; it produces an ugly flaw in a novel which, until the grafted-on happy ending, had been an excellent one.

But, in symbolic as distinguished from realistic fiction, the same idea may be dramatized without any such flaw. MacDonald may, as he does with some of the maimed creatures in *Lilith,* invent a posthumous Other World in which those whom God had insufficient time to reward in this life are given an extension of time beyond the grave; in this indefinite future their reward may come *even if the story ends before the reward's achievement.* Thus at the ends of both *Phantastes* and *Lilith,* the heroes are not yet blessed but are back in this world having glimpsed the Other World in which they do not doubt that their rewards will come in time.

Time is, in fact, of the essence; in Chapter 2, I pointed out that MacDonald maintained the original and striking religious idea that God must operate in time when dealing with such time-bound creatures as men, thus necessarily setting aside His own attribute of timelessness, suspending transcendence in order to be immanent in the human world. But the realistic novel is of necessity confined to this world and may not be set in the next; thus, to argue God's eventual justice in the novel involves doing violence to plausibility, while no such disaster is inherent in fantasies which make the same point.

Furthermore, we have noted that MacDonald's true originality of thought lay, not in his social and political views, which are the domain of the novel, but rather in his religious and psychological insights, perhaps better suited to symbolic expression. An abstract, metaphysical force, such as the Platonic idea of beauty, or a psychological attribute of personality such as the unconscious, cannot realistically be *embodied* in a real person, though such an abstraction might well be *dramatized* in the conflicts undergone by such a person. But an abstraction might easily be distilled into an otherworldly being symbolizing *only* that idea, uncomplicated by the vicissitudes of the flesh. (I should not want to argue, however, that religious and psychological insights can be properly given expression only in fantasy or that social and political concepts are appropriate only in realistic fiction. Nevertheless, it is arguable that MacDonald's more original and profound ideas do lend themselves *relatively* better to expression in symbolic fantasy than they do in realism.)

Such generalizations as these are not, of course, obvious by inspection without illustration. Therefore an examination in some detail of MacDonald's symbolic practices is needed, both to show his mythopoeic imagination in action and to illustrate the nature of his characteristic Muse—the inspiration which touched almost all of his fantasies but found the novel inherently uncongenial.

II *A Vocabulary of Symbols*

Because the term "symbol" is used with such frequency in modern criticism, it need not be elaborately defined beyond saying that it refers to a person, place, object, or event which stands for some thing or some idea other than itself. Of greater usefulness in the analysis of MacDonald's practice of symbolism is the idea of distinguishing between various *kinds* of symbols found in literature, just as we distinguish between the parts of speech—for symbolism is, indeed, a kind of language. A symbol may be called, in the distinction-making terminology which I feel is needed here, traditional, natural, universal, or private.

A *traditional* symbol is one which has been assigned a purely arbitrary meaning during the course of history and has since been preserved in the ordinary course of cultural transmission. For example, in *Lilith* Mr. Vane bathes Lilith's near-dead body in a warm "river of life" which, according to Greville MacDonald, is made up of the four elements of medieval alchemy: water, air, earth, fire. This idea, of course, may be Greville MacDonald's rather than his father's conscious intention; but I suspect that the son, who was middle-aged by the time *Lilith* was written and who had frequently discussed George MacDonald's works with their author, probably knew his father's mind in this case. The elements are endowed with symbolic significance according to the esoteric mysticism of Jacob Boehme, from whom MacDonald apparently borrowed the whole idea.

Greville MacDonald informs us that "The metallic taste of the water stands for Earth, the heat of it is for Fire, the river itself for Water; while the Air-element is known by the 'bluish mist that rose from it, vanishing as it rose.' " [1] The elements are related to Boehme's esoteric symbolism as follows: "In Boehme's teaching, they correspond with the four temperaments, 'the four chambers of the Soul's Inn': Fire with the choleric, Air with the sanguine, Water with the phlegmatic, and Earth with the melancholic." [2] The "traditional" or arbitrary nature of the symbolism is clear enough: there is no *inherent* reason for the correspondence of the elements with the "humours," nor for the correspondence in turn of the "humours" with the alleged varieties of temperament.

In fact, what Greville MacDonald, or Boehme himself, might see in the river is of little actual literary value in *Lilith*, because the tradition involved is an outmoded medieval psychology which has been largely forgotten by the reading public. On the other hand, some traditional symbols are still alive: the cross, for instance, is a powerful symbol associated with Jesus, though there is no *inherent* correspondence between the symbol and the thing symbolized. The cross might be meaningless to an Asian native who has escaped the attentions of Christian missionaries, but in the Western world it is a living traditional symbol, an association which occurs in history and has become established in Christian tradition.

The practitioner of symbolic technique is on psychologically firmer ground when there *is* an inherent correspondence, in at least one respect, between the symbol and the idea symbolized. Perhaps the most familiar example of this sort is the identification of the metamorphosis of a caterpillar into a butterfly with the transfiguration of the soul at death; the word *psyche* was, in fact, used by the ancient Greeks to mean *both* "soul" and "butterfly." MacDonald makes frequent and effective use of this second kind of symbol, which I call *natural,* as illustrated by another passage from *Lilith:*

> The sun broke through the clouds, and the raindrops flashed and sparkled on the grass. The raven walked over it. . . .
> "You will wet your feet!" I cried.
> "And mire my beak," he answered, immediately plunging it deep in the sod, and drawing out a great wriggling red worm. He threw back his head, and tossed it in the air. It spread great wings, gorgeous in red and black, and soared aloft.
> "Tut! Tut!" I exclaimed; "You mistake, Mr. Raven: worms are not the larvae of butterflies!" [3]

Mr. Vane's pedantic objection is interesting: the transformation of a *caterpillar* into a butterfly naturally suggests the beatification of the soul after death in cultures where the idea of the soul exists, as it did in Greece, but this is a *worm.* The Bible repeatedly refers to man as a worm (Job 25:6: "How much less man, that is a worm; and the son of man, which is a worm"). Perhaps MacDonald meant to emphasize that even the more wormlike, ignoble aspects of man's nature need not prevent his transformation. To me, there is still another association involving the word *worm;* I think of the snake in Eden, possibly because the Old English noun *wyrma* is used indiscriminately for both snakes and earthworms; I therefore associate this passage with MacDonald's belief that Satan, too, will ultimately be transformed and redeemed. I cannot assert that MacDonald himself made the same private association, but I offer this instance as an example of the peculiar suggestive resonance of which MacDonald's symbolism is so often capable.

Both traditional and natural symbolism are culturally conditioned: the former depends entirely upon a culturally transmitted association of the symbol with the thing symbolized even though there is no inherent similarity between the two; the latter, upon the prior existence in a culture of an idea which is naturally and automatically seen to correspond with some attribute of the symbol for it. But there is a third class of symbols which is independent of culture, independent both of arbitrary associations traditionally inherited (earth equals black bile equals melancholy) and more natural correspondences conditioned by culture in that the idea symbolized may not be universal (butterfly equals soul). The worm is also a symbol of death, by an apparent if grisly association; and death, unlike the idea of the soul, *is* universal. The worm-butterfly passage from *Lilith,* then, also involves a third kind of symbolism, which I call *universal* symbolism, involving an automatic and obvious association independent of culture.

The presence within this one brief passage of three different orders of symbolism—traditional, natural, and universal—endows it with a richness of meaning which embodies one of MacDonald's metaphysical or religious doctrines far more neatly and concentratedly than a declarative statement could. It suggests not only that we sinners (worms) may be transfigured (metamorphosis) but also that death (worms in another context) is not an end—since the worm enters a new life as a butterfly—but a means or a passage to redemption. This is not to say, of course, that such a complex of meaning is manifest out of context, but this symbolic event is embodied within an imaginative work which, at one time or another, makes each of those points separately: therefore, it serves to reinforce them all.

In the fourth kind of symbolism, which I call *private* for want of a better word, the association between the symbol and the thing symbolized is by no means obvious and inevitable; but neither is it entirely arbitrary or dependent upon culture. It is something which its user has seen *in propria persona* and that he has established as an identification through the operation of its autobiographical significance. In the fascinating study *The Poetic Mind*, Frederick Clarke Prescott cites a typical instance of private symbolism: "A. W. Schlegel found a symbolism in sounds, and regarded *a* as suggestive of bright red, and conveying youth, joy, or brightness (as in the words *Strahl, Glanz*). He may in this way have got genuine effects of 'tone color' from poetry, which others, lacking the same associations, cannot share." [4]

Such a private symbolic phenomenon is MacDonald's favorite motif of the library in an upper-class mansion, a setting which occurs in both novels and fantasies. The meaning of the library is inherently obscure—all we know is that it must have meant something intensely significant to MacDonald since it occurs so frequently. Certainly, it originates with the library which MacDonald catalogued during his vacation from Aberdeen University, but we do not know exactly what happened there. It is possible in such cases to reason backward and treat the work of fiction as autobiographical, though the procedure must be used with due caution in the absence of definite biographical facts. It is safe to say, for instance, that in that northern library MacDonald must first have come upon the works of the German Romantics who influenced him so profoundly: the protagonist of *The Portent* undergoes the same experience. It is even possible to conjecture that MacDonald may have fallen in love with the daughter of the house, for his heroes usually do so when employed as librarians. Professor Wolff rather rashly *insists* that it happened that way.

Such presumably autobiographical episodes cannot be termed "symbolic" unless an author manages to infuse them with a *feeling* of intense meaningfulness more powerful than whatever import they derive from their mere narrative function. MacDonald does so with his libraries, but we sometimes cannot tell what they "mean," though we feel that they mean *something* intensely.

Sometimes the library suggests the liberating power of knowledges; sometimes it seems (as in *Lilith,* where Mr. Raven is both librarian and sexton) to be a repository for the souls of the dead great. In such cases it may be said that, for the author who uses them, private symbols are more important than what they stand for. Their meaning is arbitrary, as is true of traditional symbols, but they differ from the traditional in that they originate in the writer's own life rather than in his cultural heritage.

III   *The Symbolic Artist's Personality*

The mere appearance of all four kinds of symbols in MacDonald's fantasies means little by itself. No doubt any writer can plant symbols if he finds them useful or if, as is true today, they are fashionable. MacDonald's special gift lies rather in the fact that his symbolism is powerful and resonant, as in the case of the worm-butterfly-death-transfiguration complex which I have cited. That incident from *Lilith* is, furthermore, nothing more than an incident—MacDonald simply drops it into his story and then forgets about it. What the occurrence of such phenomena on nearly every page does prove is that symbolism was for MacDonald a habitual language. It is as if his Muse whispered into his ear not in plain words but in evocative images which he dutifully transcribed when he was writing in the appropriate medium. Less metaphorically, it may be observed that George MacDonald was of a personality type which predisposed him to such language.

It need hardly be argued that different kinds of writers have different kinds of personalities. It must have struck every student of literature at one time or another that there is something about Shakespeare, Browning, and Thackeray that makes them different from Blake, Shelley, and Kafka. And it immediately strikes anyone who has read this far that MacDonald belongs in the latter group rather than in the former. Yet it is equally clear that MacDonald's conventional novels are, or attempt to be, in the realistic tradition. While he might be as fine a symbolic writer as Kafka, nobody would place him on a level of excellence with Thackeray as a realist.

The subject of the artist's personality-type has not been very thoroughly studied. It has been frequently observed that Shakespeare wrote about practically every personality-type except the mystic, but few critics have tried to explain why. The best study of the artistic personality I know is Frederick Clarke Prescott's *The Poetic Mind*. It was Prescott's conviction that all great artists are akin in having a tendency to see the universal and spiritual as the ultimate reality, as distinguished from the particular and worldly, the sensual and concrete. This insistence upon the superiority of the generalizing mind led Prescott into frequent absurdities—for instance, efforts to make a kind of mystic out of Dickens —but it also enabled him to distinguish the two sorts of personalities more clearly than any other critic I know of.

The Poetic Mind contains a brilliant analysis of how the personality-type into which MacDonald falls functions in art. Prescott makes the distinction in this way: "It is characteristic of the imaginative mode of thought,—of the phantasy as I have called it— and of poetry as one of its products, that compared with voluntary thought, it is less individual and limited, more general and nearer to the universal and the absolute." [5] Prescott then explores the arrangement of events in time and its dislocation in what he calls "poetry" and what I call "imaginative literature":

In ordinary thought, we think within the forms of time and space. . . . Primitive man, first exercising this thought and seeking food or defense, would have found it necessary immediately to fix such relations. With the development of his senses he learned to perceive immediate duration and extent, and he presently advanced from these to the conception of general time and space. . . . To the practical life, individual or social, these two charts of time and space, upon which all impressions may be located, are indispensable.

But while ordinary thought is thus rigorously subject to these temporal and spatial conditions, thought of the other order is not. The two charts are modified, distorted, and even, in a sense, dispensed with. . . .

Time is nothing to the visionary; he forgets about it, has no sense of its lapse, and is conscious only of its present images.[6]

Prescott cites this testimony of Shelley: "A poet participates in the eternal, the infinite, and the one; as far as relates to his conceptions, time and place and number are not. The grammatical forms which express the moods of time, and the differences of persons and the distinction of place, are convertible with respect to the highest poetry without injuring it as poetry." [7]

In other words, the creator's imagination forgets the laws of this world and dispenses with "mere" realism. Everywhere it sees the general, the universal, the one behind the many; it *must* ignore the laws of this world in order to see the "more absolute" world of Platonic ideas, the "white radiance of eternity" behind the obscuring and distorting "dome of many-colored glass" which is ordinary life, the life of the senses, of time and place. To cite Prescott again, "Ordinary thought has greater immediate grasp and deftness, but obviously it must secure this advantage by a limitation and a compensating loss of freedom." [8] In short, the writer of symbolic fantasy is "free" of the "limitations" inherent in the laws of this world. If he tries, as MacDonald did in his novels, to confine himself within those laws, the result is likely to be failure.

In discussing the genres of fiction in his monumental *Anatomy of Criticism,* Northrop Frye suggests the same sort of distinction between kinds of artistic imagination, and he parallels them with the kinds of fiction written by artists of the two kinds; but Frye is wiser than Prescott in seeing that there *can* be artists of the particularizing as well as of the generalizing sort:

> When we start to think seriously about the novel, not as fiction, but as a form of fiction, we feel that its characteristics, whatever they are, are such as make, say, Defoe, Fielding, Austen, and James central in its tradition, and Borrow, Peacock, Melville, and Emily Brontë somehow peripheral. . . . The shape of the plot is different: instead of manoeuvering around a central situation, as Jane Austen does, Emily Brontë tells her story with linear accents, and she seems to need the help of a narrator, who would be absurdly out of place in Jane Austen. Conventions so different justify us in regarding *Wuthering Heights* as a different form of prose fiction from the novel, a form which we shall here call the romance. . . .
>
> The essential difference between the novel and the romance lies in the conception of characterization. The romancer does not attempt to create "real people" so much as stylized figures which expand into psychological archetypes. It is in the romance that we find Jung's libido, anima, and shadow reflected in the hero, heroine, and villain respectively. . . . The novelist deals with . . . characters wearing their *personae* or social masks. He needs the framework of a stable society, and many of our best novelists have been conventional to the verge of fussiness. The romancer deals with . . . characters *in vacuo* idealized by reverie.[9]

So much for the distinction between artistic personality types and for the kinds of characters likely to be envisioned by the two types of personality described by Prescott and Frye. But what of plot and setting, the other two members (besides character) of the serviceable triad which I have already made use of in chapters 3 and 4? And what of MacDonald's works as illustrations of the kinds of characters, plots, and settings found in both conventional realistic novels and what Frye calls "romance," what Prescott calls simply "poetry," and what I call by such names as "imaginative fiction," "symbolic narrative," "fantasy," and "mythopoeia"?

IV *Fantasy Characters as Archetypes*

In Chapter 3, I pointed out that the characters in MacDonald's realistic novels strike the reader as banal "stereotypes" rather than as "real people." As Frye suggests, idealized heroes, heroines, and villains are somehow appropriate in the "romance" but inappropriate in the novel. Yet MacDonald was, when he perpetrated his stereotyped and banal characterizations, *trying* to write conventional realistic novels, to observe the laws of this world as they really are, to place his characters in a realistic social context, and to observe what Prescott calls the conventions of sequential time and oriented space.

Generally, MacDonald fails in this aim in his novels. When we meet a nasty landlord consciously and deliberately motivated by lust and greed, we complain that real people are too complex to be like that; that real human beings are not so simply constituted as to be simplistic. We should not complain at meeting the Essence of Evil in a dream world, but we are offended by MacDonald's unrealistic, simplistic insistence that it takes unalloyed human shape in the waking world. (Shakespeare, who unlike MacDonald saw solid people rather than types, tried to invent totally black villains and failed in that he made Malvolio, Shylock, and perhaps even Iago too human to be "stagey" villains.) It is evident that Prescott is speaking of writers like MacDonald in describing a kind of imagination which *always* sees the general, even when it is not really there.

MacDonald's tendency to see the general in character is probably the reason for his manufacture of stereotypes in the novel; in the fantasy, however, the same tendency produces what Frye calls "archetypes." An archetypal character is one who appears throughout the history of imaginative literature; and, unlike the stereotype of bad realistic literature, he strikes the reader in a powerful and evocative way. Jung, who uses the term "archetype" to signify an invented personality which represents a projection in fantasy of a constituent element of the self, suggests that we all have a "collective unconscious" world populated by characters who are essentially the same since they represent universal elements of human experience.

For example, we have fathers who usually live long enough for us to know them. Even if they do not, we acquire from contact with our peers the idea that the father is ideally the repository of all wisdom, and the source of advice to the child who is trying to learn about the world. Unfortunately, our real fathers usually fail us in this respect or are not so all-wise as their familial role demands that they be. Therefore, we invent an imaginary perfect father who inhabits our wish-fulfillment dreams as the archetype of the Wise Old Man. The appearance of such a figure in imaginative literature produces in us a "shock of recognition" because we *have* met him before in our dreams. Construed as a symbol, he stands for the wisdom, the source of conscience, and the intermediary between ourselves and the universe which we sought and failed to find in our own fathers. The Wise Old Man is part of our souls.

Jung's theory of the archetypes of the collective unconscious is, of course, merely a construct—a hypothetical formula for explaining how such characters get into everybody's dream life in the first place and why their appearance in literature affects us so powerfully. The literary critic lacks the psychoanalyst's clinical experience and must hesitate to affirm any literal belief in the alleged collective unconscious, but the critic is at least able to recognize a plausible idea when he sees one. Jung's theory has impressed an entire generation of literary critics, and his literary effects may well outlast his effect on what is at present still the pseudoscience of psychology. Speaking as a critic, I am happy to adopt Jung's terminology to refer to literary phenomena which need names and to leave its status as "science" to the scientists.

George MacDonald's symbolic fantasies are, then, full of archetypal characters, all of which may be identified with those which Jung has catalogued by collating the dreams and fantasies of his patients. One of them, "the Shadow," he defined as "the dangerous aspect of the unrecognized dark half of the personality." [10] Our ego hates to admit that there is evil in us, so we banish its embodiment to the unconscious, allowing it to face us in dreams as if it were separate from ourselves. In defining "the Shadow", Jung also finds a number of its qualities which strike the reader as applicable to certain of MacDonald's characters: "Closer examination of the dark characteristics—that is, the inferiorities constituting the shadow—reveals that they have an *emotional* nature, a kind of *autonomy*, and accordingly an *obsessive* or, better, *possessive* quality."[11]

I have no idea where Jung found his name for what he calls "the Shadow," but it is a fascinating coincidence that George Mac-Donald uses precisely the same term for the same character. In *Phantastes*, for example, Anodos acquires a black Shadow which spoils everything beautiful for him. At one point, he meets a little girl who carries a lovely globe; but, when the Shadow falls upon the globe, the fragile thing shatters, and the child runs away in terror. Interpreted symbolically, the Shadow refers specifically to the monster of lust which shatters and spoils love—the shattering of the globe naturally evoking the idea of defloration in our minds. An even more striking instance of the same idea occurs in *Lilith* where the "villain" is a disembodied, sinister spirit called the Shadow, who haunts the streets of the corrupt city of Bulika and afflicts Lilith herself with a sort of obsessive disfigurement. In her alternate manifestation as a leopard, Lilith is spotted; and, when she appears as a woman, she has a shadowy spot on her side. Lilith's unwillingness to surrender her disfigurement for fear of losing her identity is an instance of the "obsessiveness" identified by Jung as a characteristic of the Shadow.

A comparable mechanism accounts for the presence in a man's unconscious of a character whom Jung calls the Anima: the unrecognized female part of the male personality that is denied because to admit its presence would seem "unmanly." The Anima is associated, in effect, with *all* of a man's women:

> In the case of the son, the projection-making factor is identified with the *mother imago*, and this is consequently taken to be the real mother. The projection can only be resolved when he comes to realize that in the realm of his psyche there exists an image of the mother and not only of the mother, but also of the daughter, the sister, the beloved, the heavenly goddess, and the earth spirit. . . . It is his own, this perilous image of Woman; she stands for the loyalty which in the interests of life he cannot always maintain; she is the vital

compensation for the risks, the struggles, the sacrifices which all end
in disappointment; she is the solace for all the bitterness of life.
Simultaneously, she is the great illusionist, the seductress who draws
him into life—not only into its reasonable and useful aspects but into
its frightful paradoxes and ambivalences where good and evil, success
and ruin, hope and despair counterbalance one another.[12]

Obviously, since this figure contains both the terrifying and the
vivifying aspects of woman, she is inclined to break in two. As
protective mother, she is the Wise Old Woman, the fairy godmother, or, in MacDonald, "grandmother"; as temptress, she is the
succuba, a female demon who appears to a man in his sleep and
seduces him, to his horror and waking guilt.

Lilith, herself, when she is not the helpless victim of the
Shadow, appears as a classic embodiment of the Succuba-Anima.
At one point in *Lilith,* Mr. Vane has been sleeping in the prin-
cess's castle:

When I opened my eyes, it was night. . . . A delicious languor
enfolded me. I seemed floating, far from land, upon the bosom of a
twilight sea. Existence was in itself pleasure. I had no pain. Surely I
was dying!

No pain!—ah, what a shoot of mortal pain was that! what a sickening sting! It went right through my heart! Again! That was sharp-
ness itself!—and so sickening! I could not move my hand to lay it on
my heart; something kept it down!

The pain was dying away, but my whole body seemed paralysed.
Some evil thing was upon me!—something hateful! I would have
struggled, but I could not reach a struggle. My will agonised, but in
vain, to assert itself. I desisted, and lay passive. Then I became aware
of a soft hand on my face, pressing my head into the pillow, and of
a heavy weight lying across me.

I began to breathe more freely; the weight was gone from my
chest; I opened my eyes.

The princess was standing above me on the bed, looking out into
the room, with the air of one who dreamed. Her great eyes were clear
and calm. Her mouth wore a look of satisfied passion; she wiped from
it a streak of red.[13]

Certainly this portrayal is a compelling rendition of an erotic
dream, after which the unfortunate victim, now awake, feels guilt-
ily that he has been raped by a malevolent demon. An odd aspect
of the incident is that Lilith does not assume the conventional

woman's role since she violates the ever-passive Mr. Vane and
since she, on top of him, is the aggressor. In this respect she resembles other assaulting, bloodsucking vampire women among
MacDonald's characters (such as the otherwise uninteresting female vampire in "The Grey Wolf"), although I have not seen
vampirism elsewhere considered as a specifically female archetypal idea; most literary vampires are males. Perhaps in this respect vampirism could be said to symbolize that aspect of woman
which robs man of his bachelor freedom and is jealous of his attention to his work (as MacDonald's wife was jealous of his devotion to his God). There is no need, however, to go on perpetrating
Freudian and Jungian excesses in an oracular tone; the rape scene
in *Lilith* is a powerful one, and that after all is the literary fact,
whatever its psychoanalytical explanation may be.

Occasionally, MacDonald tells us about an Old Witch (as distinguished from either a benevolent old woman or a malevolent
young one); she is an Evil Old Woman straight from traditional
fairy tales. This nasty figure usually embodies the old woman's
jealousy of a young girl's beauty and fertility. MacDonald's most
effective Old Witch is the one in "The Light Princess," who, like
the evil witch in *Snow White and the Seven Dwarfs*, hates and
curses the young female protagonist. But, since there are few female protagonists in MacDonald's work (Curdie is the real protagonist of *The Princess and the Goblin* and *The Princess and
Curdie*), it is hardly surprising that MacDonald depicts few
witches.

Barbara Catanach, the evil old midwife in *Malcolm* and *The
Marquis of Lossie*, is, in fact, the only one of MacDonald's villains
in the realistic fiction who is really convincing; and she is a sort of
witch rather than a real person or a stereotype. A character from a
literature alien to the novel, she is another indication of the arbi-
trariness of any pat division of fiction into the realistic and the
fantastic. There is surely a middle ground between the archreal-
ism of a Trollope and the archsymbolism of a Dante, and it is here
that some of the masters of fiction—Melville and Emily Brontë,
for instance—fit in the subcategory which Frye calls Romance.
What is striking is that MacDonald never really occupied this
middle ground, for Bauby Catanach is almost the only character
who would be at home in the Gothic stories of Poe or among the
grotesques of Dickens; she is, in fact, a sort of female Fagin. Most

of MacDonald's characters, in contrast, are either realistic stereotypes or symbolic archetypes. He rarely achieves, as Melville almost always does, a blending of the two: characters too human to
be an archetype; too weird to be a stereotype; too peculiar to be
like the man who is mowing his lawn next door.

A final Jungian archetype of imaginative fiction and dreams is
the *libido,* the desiring aspect of the self, the quester, the adven-
turing and conquering hero, by means of which we conquer and
possess. Again a person tries to separate this victor from himself
through "projection," for it is hard to admit that he can be so
greedy. Here we generally look in vain among MacDonald's fantasies for an archetypal *libido* character: Anodos and Mr. Vane
are too flawed, frustrated, and passive to fit the mold, but perhaps
Curdie comes close. Perhaps the general absence of a pure *libido*
hero in MacDonald is a reflection of his remarkable self-aware-
ness: he recognized the *libido* as a wish-fulfillment projection and
therefore resisted any temptation to make his hero all-conquering.
Wolff, of course, believes that MacDonald was *not* conscious of
his own natural tendencies toward projection, and he would probably disagree with me, though I should like to see him find an
explanation of the absence of supermen in MacDonald's
fantasies.

Thus, Jung postulates the existence of a whole cast of characters
in the dream world of everyone: the Wise Old Man, the Shadow,
the Succuba-Anima, her counterpart the Wise Old Woman, the
Libido. Our sense of symmetry can provide us with a few others:
the Rival Male for men, the Animus for women, and so forth. The
significant quality in all of these archetypal characters is that they
appear almost automatically in any work of genuine fantasy, just
as their existence in our dreams is unconditioned by our will. Each
is a generalization of character which is also a projection into fantasy of some (usually unwelcome) aspect of our own personalities. That nearly every one of them appears in MacDonald's works
is yet another indication that his was a generalizing imagination
—one at home in fantasy and lost or incongruous or banal in the
world of the novel, the rational re-creation of waking life.

V *Fantasy-Plots as Myths*

Jung usually confines his concept of the archetype to characterization, but we might also expect to find generalized types of

plot and setting. I have, in fact, already noted Frye's opinion that what he considers Romance seems more congenial to a "linear" plot than to "manoeuvering about a central situation" as is Jane Austen's plot-making practice. It thus seems reasonable to find a term which pins down the generalized plot as the term "archetype" describes the generalized character found in fantasy. In Chapter 3, I complained that the plots of MacDonald's novels are inclined to be as banal as his characters: boy-meets-girl, boy-grows-up-and-finds-God, and so forth. Again the formulaic plot is annoying rather than enriching when it appears in the novel, but it is powerful and striking when it provides the story-line of fantasy.

Certainly there is no more universal and "typical" fantasy-plot than the Journey to the Other World (*Phantastes, Lilith, At the Back of the North Wind,* "The Golden Key"). And again the "shock of recognition" strikes us in fantasy as a revelation because it is so like our own dream-life, while such simplicities seem "unreal" in the novel because our waking lives, with which realism by its very nature begs to be compared, are decidedly not that simple. A desire to be systematic prompts me to look for a name for the generalized plot as it appears in fantasy, as distinguished from the term "formula" applied to plot-clichés in the novel. I suggest, therefore, that we already have such a name in the term *myth,* which has been immemorially used to describe entire schemes of events.

I am indebted to the late Professor C. S. Lewis for the idea that the term *myth* is to be applied to a pattern of events which appears repeatedly in stories which have referential meaning beyond their literal surface significance. Lewis suggests that "Orpheus loses Eurydice by looking back at her too soon, and this is like spoiling a pleasure by trying to introspect it, *and* like losing a virtue (e.g., humility) by becoming aware that we have it, *and* like the destruction of an incipient love-affair by recognizing (too soon or in the wrong way) that it *is* love, *and* like St. Peter's sinking because he noticed that he was walking on water—*and* so on *and* so on." [14]

We need not multiply instances of the mythic plot, as I have done in showing how precisely MacDonald's cast of generalized characters corresponds with Jung's list of archetypes; for, ordinarily, there are only a few typical myth-plots, of which MacDonald himself utilized still fewer. Other such plots are the universal stories of the flood or other natural disasters designed by God to exterminate a sinful race and of the messianic savior who comes to redeem the righteous. It is no accident that such stories, which Westerners tend to identify with specifically Judeo-Christian culture, are paralleled in the literatures of non-Western cultures such as those of the American Indians, the Polynesians, and others. Most such "myths" are primitive attempts to explain the metaphysical nature of human life, just as the Garden of Eden myth "explains" man's fallen nature; and thus myths are usually religious in import.

MacDonald's characteristic plot-myth is the search for a divine unity, an unrealized but hoped-for goal. We note that Anodos, Mr. Vane, and Mossy and Tangle never quite attain their objectives, though through their adventures on the way they get closer. As I have suggested, MacDonald's predilection for the chain-adventure story, as Auden calls it, and for the journey, as Evelyn Underhill terms it, represents his own personal religious preoccupation with "the Mystic Way," the individual's journey toward God. MacDonald's fantasy heroes at least make *some* progress, though they never quite arrive; by contrast, Kafka's typical myth is the confrontation between the searching protagonist and the authority of the mysterious and transcendent Other in which the protagonist fails and is defeated.

VI   *Fantasy Settings as Symbols*

Finally, and even more briefly, we may establish a convenient terminology for the settings of MacDonald's fantasies. A setting is a place, a thing rather than a person (archetype) or a chain of events (myth). The image of the uncharted, many-chambered house is probably as old as the caveman and as universal in man's dreams as any of the already-mentioned elements of character and plot. We may term the referentially meaningful setting a *symbol*, since that term usually (but not always) is applied to *things* which mean something other than their literal meaning, just as MacDonald's uncharted castle is like a mind with its unexplored chambers and many levels of awareness.

The term *symbol* is often used in criticism rather loosely; it is applied to *anything* which signifies something beyond its literal meaning. Thus criticism talks of "symbolic" characters and plots, as well as about "symbolic" places and things. But most literary symbols *are* places and things—in other words, elements of setting. I may be straining for "fearful symmetry" here, but not too desperately since MacDonald *does* repeat typical settings and since they *do* mean typical ideas. The Wasteland, as I have noted, is uniquely identified in MacDonald's fantasies with the absence of tears and with children who refuse to grow up ("The Light Princess" and *Lilith*); but in Arthurian and pagan literature, as in Eliot's *The Waste Land*, the same setting's dearth of water represents sterility in a sexual rather than a maturational sense, so that water is perhaps identified with semen rather than with tears.

VII *The Problem of "Intention"*

Myth, archetype, symbol—plot, character, setting—journey-to-the-other world, Anima, the many-chambered house—such a critical scheme is admittedly an artifact, something made in a sense by the critic rather than by the author; but it seems useful, the ultimate test of any artifact. Applied to the works of George Mac-Donald, this scheme suggests everywhere the same thing: Mac-Donald's mind was superbly suited to the imaginative fiction for which he has been repeatedly praised by modern critics; but it was inherently alien to the specific, particular, worldly, sensual, existential, temporal, spatial, moral, social, and political world of the realistic novel.

Yet there is something peculiar about MacDonald, something which distinguishes him from most practitioners of imaginative fiction. It is clear, for instance, that he may not have consciously "intended" to say some of the things that he undoubtedly does say—or, at least, he did not expect his Victorian readers to understand some of the sexual symbolism which the post-Freudian reader sees in such works as "The Light Princess" or *Wilfrid Cumbermede*. We know that MacDonald was deliberately trying to inculcate his personal religious message in his readers. If, in the process, he struck a more universal note than even he, himself, consciously meant to strike, it only shows that his imagination was of the most powerfully generalizing sort.

But, if his "intention" was limited, his achievement was less so; and we are faced with the problem of understanding how he managed to speak so resoundingly to another generation than his own, and even to embody with great power ideas which appeal to atheists—an achievement which probably would have horrified MacDonald himself. In order to grasp MacDonald's total accomplishment, we must see both what he *meant* to do and what he *did* do; the next chapter seeks to establish the relation between MacDonald's consciously "intended" meaning and his more universal, timeless, humanly universal meaning. For, if in one sense his muse was mythic-archetypal-symbolic, it was, in another way, deliberately didactic and thus "allegorical" in purpose if not in achievement. The problem is to discover why MacDonald's specifically didactic purpose managed to transcend itself and to say so much to so many.

CHAPTER 6

The Didactic Muse

I *The Spiritual Education*

IN Chapter 2 George MacDonald's most interesting ideas were assembled into a more or less coherent scheme—something which he himself never did. In this chapter, we examine the ways he found for expressing one of those ideas, or rather a pattern of interrelated concepts, in symbolic form. The central concept to be traced throughout MacDonald's fantasies is that of his viewing man's life as a stepwise process of cumulative enlightenment, a sort of spiritual education in which a man passes from one "grade" to another.

MacDonald's concept of the spiritual education involves several of his most characteristic and original views. It is the result, for one thing, of his conviction that God, when dealing with men, is limited since He can do His work only in time, thus abandoning one of His primary attributes—timelessness, God's existence in eternity. MacDonald's chain of reasoning led him to postulate that, after this life, we may have to pass through a whole series of probationary states on the way to ultimate enlightenment; for earthly life is too short for the completion of an education. Thus, death is simply one more "graduation" into a "higher grade."

Another aspect of this subject concerns *how* man learns. One way is to study the language of correspondences by which God has given man clues to His meaning; the man skilled in seeing the eternal Idea behind a limited, physical object has the means to understand more than the man who has not yet developed this faculty, or has not learned the language. A second means of learning is through the mystic insights which God grants to some; but that type of direct perception is not available except at the "graduate level"—that is, it is a discipline requiring a long preparatory apprenticeship. A third source of spiritual truth is dreams as hints of the future or as suggestions of the laws of the next world and the one after that. Finally, for those who are still in the "elemen-tary grades," the surest way to "move up" or "be promoted" is simply to *do,* as well as they can, that little which they know how to do; for, in the process of doing they ready themselves for new knowledge.

Even in thus briefly summarizing the idea, I have found myself resorting to a metaphor, treating the entire process as if it were an educational curriculum from grade school through graduate study, presided over by a sort of divine board of education. The idea lends itself nicely to analogy with less metaphysical and more concrete and familiar phenomena. MacDonald himself felt that his message was difficult; therefore, he consciously sought to drive it home by whatever means he could find. His sermons are full of direct attempts to explain what he meant, but he knew that few people want to read sermons or to concentrate on their philoso-phical content. His novels at least reached a wider audience; yet, when he dramatized this idea in conventional fiction, MacDonald could apparently think of nothing better than to interpolate still more sermons and disquisitions into his stories, with, as we have noted, deadly results. Fortunately, he hit upon the symbolic way to insinuate the concept into his reader's mind without, perhaps, the reader's ever being quite aware that he was being subtly in-structed; and it is in this area that MacDonald's deliberate didac-ticism was most successful, both intellectually and artistically.

The purpose of this chapter, then, is to show some of the ways with which MacDonald expressed the concept of man's spiritual education in symbolic language. Furthermore, the symbols, myths, and archetypes which he uses for this purpose have levels of meaning often quite different from what MacDonald con-sciously had in mind. It may be pointed out here that I am not necessarily perpetrating what modern critics call the "intentional fallacy" in ascribing specific intended meanings to artistic works, because we *do* know that MacDonald's "intention" was didactic, and we *do* know what he meant to say.

II *The Journey*

An obvious way of embodying the concept of the spiritual edu-cation is by use of the mythic plot-pattern of a journey. In this connection it may be observed that the myth of the journey is one of the characteristic images utilized in the literature of mysticism and summarized in the phrase "the mystic way." In her classic study, *Mysticism,* Evelyn Underhill maintains that different kinds of mystics see things in different images, of which the journey toward enlightenment is only one: "According . . . to whether man's instinct prompts him to describe . . . Absolute Reality . . . as a Place, a Person, or a State . . . so will he tend to adopt a symbolism of one or another of these three types. . . . Those who conceive the Perfect as . . . exterior to themselves and very far off . . . will feel the process of their entrance into reality to be a quest, an arduous journey from the material to the spiritual world. . . . For them, the soul is outward bound toward its home." [1]

In this sense, the simple plot-structure which involves a trip to or through the Other World can be said to correspond to the mystic's journey toward knowledge—and thus to the spiritual education which I am here using as an example of MacDonald's symbolic embodiment of his ideas. It is worth observing that most conventional fairy tales are set in an "unreal" fantasy-world from beginning to end, but that in MacDonald there is usually a transition from this world to the other that is analogous to "promotion" from one grade to another or, implicitly, to death. Although *The Princess and the Goblin* and its sequel are set entirely in fairyland, both *Phantastes* and *Lilith* involve having the protagonist begin in this world and go to fairyland through some uncanny alteration. In *Phantastes,* Anodos starts to dress in his bedroom but finishes in another world; in *Lilith,* Mr. Vane follows the apparition of his grandfather's librarian, Mr. Raven, up the stairs of his house and into the attic where he finds a mirror and steps through it into a green field. In "The Golden Key," Mossy seeks the end of the rainbow and suddenly finds himself in an alien country where the rest of the story takes place. *At the Back of the North Wind* and *Lilith* are different, as I have pointed out, in that their protagonists return to this world and go back again—in *Lilith* this sequence happens several times.

The mere transition between worlds cannot perhaps be called a journey-plot in itself, for it is only one event, only *one* "graduation," analogous to death—the passage from his world into the next—or to sleep—the passage into the world of dreams where marvelous things are revealed to us. But MacDonald never stops with the transition. When his protagonist is in the Other World, it turns out to be only the first step in his journey. Mr. Vane is immediately invited to sleep in the tombs supervised by Mr. Raven, but he cannot as yet bring himself to lie down and leaves for "somewhere." Little Diamond joins North Wind in her wanderings, but it takes him some time to reach the country at her back which is his goal. Mossy goes through fairyland in search of the keyhole which his golden key will fit; but, even after he finds it, he discovers that he has another objective: to find "the country from whence the shadows fall." At the end of the story he and Tangle are walking up the rainbow, still searching for that country. MacDonald ends the story with a conjecture: "And by this time I think they must have got there."

We may note that MacDonald's treatment of the journey-myth is unusual in several respects. The returns to this world in *At the Back of the North Wind* and in *Lilith* signify, perhaps, that flashes of mystic insight are only temporary states that are followed, rather depressingly, by relapses into the humdrum limited state of consciousness from which they had been such ecstatic escapes. We are reminded of the ending of Keats's "Ode to a Nightingale" in which the poet is tolled back from the other world of the bird to his sole self, and he wonders whether his transcendent experience was real or not. A second characteristic of MacDonald's peculiar handling of the journey myth is that his works rarely end in fulfillment—in the actual achievement of the journey's goal. "The Golden Key" ends in conjecture only, *Lilith* ends with a wiser Mr. Vane back in this world awaiting death, and *Phantastes* ends with Anodos awakening on the morning of his twenty-first birthday, with most of a lifetime yet to live in this world. All of the protagonists are wiser at the end, but have not attained ultimate wisdom, and have other future "grades" to pass through. MacDonald's departure from the tradition of journey-plots which *do* end in fulfillment is, no doubt, a reflection of his concept of the spiritual education, which in this world is a process, not an achievement.

The most striking of MacDonald's journey-myths is the plot of *Phantastes*. When Anodos awakes in fairyland, he finds himself following a river: "I crossed the rivulet, and accompanied it, keeping to the footpath on its right bank, until it led me, as I expected, into the wood. Here I left it, without any good reason, and with a vague feeling that I ought to have followed its course: I took a more southerly direction." [2] Upon first reading this passage, we are likely to think that the specific references to the *right* bank of the stream and to the *southerly* direction of Anodos's departure from it are gratuitous pieces of information designed, perhaps, to add a feeling of authenticity to the narrative. But, if we try to visualize the journey, we are following the right bank of a stream with the current; we leave the stream without jumping over it; and, if we are going south after this change of direction, then the direction of the river's flow must have been eastward.

The significance of the eastward direction becomes clearer at the beginning of the next passage: "The trees, which were far apart when I entered, giving free passage to the level rays of the rising sun, closed rapidly as I advanced, so that ere long their crowded stems barred the sunlight out, forming, as it were, a thick grating between me and the east." [3] Shortly after thus permitting himself to wander from what *should* have been a steady eastward course, Anodos experiences the first of his unpleasant adventures in fairyland—the one in which he acquires the shadow which haunts him thereafter. Not until he is again going east does he again begin to prosper, and the pattern continues throughout the story. Whenever he deviates to the south or north, disaster occurs.

It should be remembered that *Phantastes* is a twenty-one-day journey through the Other World, and that it begins on the eve of the protagonist's twenty-first birthday. Its scheme, then, is related to the process of growing up, or getting an education. And, since the name of Anodos means "a way back," the suggestion is that he is trying to find a renewal of the child's closeness to God—in accordance with MacDonald's Wordsworthian belief that in the innocence of childhood (or even near-idiocy) we are in the most direct contact with the divine. But MacDonald's ideas are not so simple as those of Wordsworth on this subject. We have also seen that "The Light Princess" and parts of *Lilith* insist that a person must *not* remain a child in his unwillingness to accept the moral responsibility and sorrow of adulthood. Childhood is not, then, an entirely ideal state in MacDonald, though it often is so painted in the works of his contemporaries. Leslie A. Fiedler, in a chapter called "The Eye of Innocence" from his volume of essays entitled *No! In Thunder* (1960, 251–91), points out the shift in the treatment of the child-archetype since the nineteenth century. In the twentieth century, the sentimentalist's view of the holy child has been reversed; the child becomes a vehicle of malice as in Vladi-

mir Nabokov's *Lolita* or William March's *The Bad Seed*. Mac-
Donald's treatment of this subject, then, may be seen as a transition from nineteenth-century sentimentalism to twentieth-century
grimness, a minor turning point in the history of Western literature.

But to return from this digression to the subject of the specifically Eastward Journey: another instance of the preferability of
taking the eastward course appears in *Lilith*. After refusing to lie
down in Mr. Raven's tombs, Mr. Vane asks him where he should
go next.

> "If I am not to go home, at least direct me to some of my kind."
> "I do not know of any. The beings most like you are in that direc-
> tion."
> He pointed with his beak. I could see nothing but the setting sun,
> which blinded me.[4]

Mr. Vane, who is only at the beginning of his spiritual education,
is ignorant. When he travels west toward the setting sun in search
of beings like himself, he soon meets the depraved Lilith and the
race of monstrous giants—creatures who share his own imperfections and corruptions. Clearly, he *should* have gone eastward, if
he had had the wit to see that Mr. Raven was mocking him, hinting that he should seek creatures *un*like himself.

The Eastward Journey has always had a special mythic meaning: it is the journey toward the source of life, toward the Asian
source of civilization, the Garden of Eden, the rising sun, Christ's
birthplace. In the psychological sense, the search for the source of
life may be considered as an introspective search for our earliest
memories and for the insights which they reveal, "a way back."
The symbolism—multiple, suggestive, indefinite—extends beyond
MacDonald's mere "intention" to incorporate all sorts of universal
levels of meaning.

It is impossible to determine whether MacDonald acquired the
symbolism of the eastward journey from William Blake or from
one of Blake's chief sources for such lore, Boehme or Swedenborg.
But there is a striking similarity between MacDonald's use of this
symbol and that of Blake in *Jerusalem,* which MacDonald is
known to have read.[5] S. Foster Damon gives a table of the "four-
fold correspondences" of *Jerusalem;* and, under the heading

"East," he lists, among others, the following meanings: Emotions, Love, Center, Inward direction, and Asia.[6]

Quite aside from eastwardness, however, MacDonald's heroes have plenty to do in the Other World. But a spiritual education must be purposeful; there must be a goal in view, or at least a *reason* for undertaking new adventures. Otherwise, adventures may become arbitrary rather than meaningful, gratuitous excitement-for-its-own-sake rather than cumulative *stages* in a continuing educational process. And in this respect W. H. Auden makes an interesting suggestion:

> If *Lilith* is a more satisfactory book than *Phantastes*, one reason is that its allegorical structure is much tighter; there seems no particular reason, one feels, why Anodos should have just the number of adventures which he does have—they could equally be more or less—but Mr. Vane's experiences and his spiritual education exactly coincide. The danger of a chain adventure story is that perpetual novelty gives excitement at the cost of understanding; the landscape of *Lilith* becomes all the more vivid and credible to the reader because he is made to repeat the journey Adam's-Cottage to Bad-Burrow to Dry-River to Evil-Wood to Orchard-Valley to Rocky-Scaur to Hot-Stream to Bulika-City several times.[7]

If we grant that the landscape in *Lilith* becomes familiar through repetition, it is at least questionable whether Mr. Vane's running in circles is more effective than the linearity of Anodos's journey—although to retrace a path so compulsively is perhaps an appropriate image for the lostness which characterizes Mr. Vane. It is as though he had to repeat a grade in school because he had failed to learn its lessons the first time.

Both the repetitiousness of Mr. Vane's wanderings and Anodos's having strayed from the ordained eastward path have symbolic implications which are analogous to the fact that Mr. Vane and Little Diamond come back from the Other World after each journey. In all of these cases, there is the suggestion that the spiritual education may not necessarily be a steady progress and that it may, in fact, be interrupted by what a Freudian would call "regressions"—lapses back into a "lower grade," or (again in terms of the school metaphor) "demotions." Since MacDonald evidently considers retrogression as a possibility, as we shall see, his scheme lends itself to analogies which involve "negative" progress. It is therefore not surprising that MacDonald selects the spatial analogy of the journey, since in journeying man may get lost and move *away from* rather than toward the goal. It is also not surprising that MacDonald does *not* make much use of the temporal, as distinguished from the spatial, dimension; for in human experience time is *not* reversible. If it were not for this factor of reversibility, we might expect MacDonald to utilize time-dependent analogies such as the morning-noon-night or spring-summer-fall-winter or phases-of-the-moon progressions. He does not, knowing that one-directional, time-oriented symbols do not correspond to his point. But MacDonald *does* find a number of other symbols for his idea of the spiritual education besides the journey-myth, which is the dominant one.

III *Other Analogies*

The analogy between taking a journey and undergoing an education is clear enough, but it is only a sampling, though the chief one, of MacDonald's catalogue of symbolic, mythic, and archetypal images for the educational process. A second such image is a typically Victorian one: the mechanism of evolution which was such a disquieting subject in that age. MacDonald was deeply concerned with keeping up with the intellectual currents of his time—as is indicated by his preoccupation with atheism, vivisection, and women's rights shown in *Paul Faber, Surgeon*. MacDonald understood the uneasy fascination with Darwinism which so disturbed his readers, and he found it another convenient means of symbolizing his ideas about the spiritual education. In *The Princess and the Goblin*, the subterranean goblins are described as descendants of men by a degenerative process which might be called "devolution." The same is true of the odd animals in *The Princess and Curdie* and of the giants in *Lilith:* all have retrogressed from previous higher ancestors.

In contrast to this retrogressive evolution, there is the growth of the air-fish in "The Golden Key"; it gives up its life as a fish in order to pass onward to a new life in a higher form. Here MacDonald's idea that the spiritual education progresses by discrete stages is obviously parallel to Darwin's discovery that, for the achievement of higher forms of life, a graduated species-by-species evolution through inferior stages is necessary. MacDonald's "contribution" to the theory of evolution, namely, the reversibility of the upward climb of species, was largely unnoticed in his own time but has been "corroborated" since around 1900 by the discovery of degenerate life forms such as the cave-dwelling fish which, though descended from species which once possessed eyesight, are now blind. It is even suspected in the mid-twentieth century that viruses are degenerate life forms which have evolved (or "devolved") from earlier species which were once nonparasitic and independent, but which have abandoned such "higher" metabolic functions as protein synthesis in the process of learning how to get their proteins made for them by their hosts. I do not claim scientific insight ahead of his time here for MacDonald, but his idea is an example of his speculative originality as conditioned by his view that degeneration, lapsing from the eastward path toward perfection, is a possibility in the scheme of the spiritual education. The idea is certainly a reflection of moral and psychological truth: human beings do degenerate, unfortunately.

Another idea implicit in the air-fish episode from "The Golden Key" is the oriental doctrine of metempsychosis—the belief that after death a soul is translated into another body which may be that of a higher or lower species, depending upon the spiritual wisdom or foolishness which the soul has shown in its last incarnation. MacDonald mentions metempsychosis several times in various sermons and stories, always in the same hesitant, speculative tone used in hinting that the devil will eventually be saved as a corollary of God's infinite mercy: he did not want to risk outright assertion of what his Christian readers might regard as heresy. Professor Wolff insists that MacDonald literally believed in metempsychosis, but such literal-mindedness seems unnecessary. Rather, it is likely that the doctrine appealed to MacDonald's imagination as a convenient symbol of his concept of the spiritual education. In addition, it accorded well with his wish—it was not quite a conviction—that the lower animals might enjoy an afterlife like man's.

Still another obvious analogy to the spiritual education may be drawn in terms of physical maturation. It, too, proceeds by stages, from infancy to childhood to adolescence to maturity to senescence to death; and it is marked by traumatic or liberating changes such as puberty, marriage, gray hair, and so forth. In "The Golden Key"—always one of the most suggestive of MacDonald's works—both Mossy and Tangle go through all the stages

of physical growth during their short stay in fairyland. Mossy
meets a number of Wise Old Men in his old age, and one of them,
The Old Man of the Sea, invites him to immerse himself in a re-
storing bath:

> "I'm not sure that I'm not old. I know my feet ache."
> "Do they?" said the Old Man . . . ; and Mossy, who was still
> lying in the bath, watched his feet for a moment before he replied.
> "No, they do not," he answered. "Perhaps I am not old either."
> He rose and looked at himself in the water, and there was not a
> gray hair on his head or a wrinkle on his skin.
> "You have tasted of death now," said the Old Man. "Is it good?"
> "It is good," said Mossy. "It is better than life."
> "No," said the Old Man: "it is only more life." [8]

Here again is the suggestion, in the use of the fountain-of-youth
motif, that the direction of the spiritual education is reversible,
and that, although in one sense greater physical maturity is to be
desired, in another sense all growth is toward the innocence of
childhood.

The necessity of maturing physically and emotionally is a recurrent motif, and it often seems to be connected specifically with the
transition of puberty. In both *Lilith* and "The Light Princess," as I
have pointed out, the necessary maturing of children is connected
with the ability to weep. The tearless children in *Lilith* live in the
Wasteland, where the absence of water in the streams is paralleled to their own lack of tears and to their persistence in childish-
ness despite the passage of time. They speak a revolting babytalk
which their creator, with typical Victorian sentimentality, apparently found sweet. Auden suggests that this language, too, is
"partly redeemed by the fact that they represent not real children
but people who, afraid of the risks and suffering involved in becoming adult, refuse to grow up." [9] They are, in other words,
cases of arrested moral development; their growth was interrupted, and the characters are frozen at a preliminary stage of
their spiritual education.

A final example of the various means by which MacDonald deliberately symbolized this central concept is perhaps the most peculiar. In *Lilith* the author is, after all, describing an invented
world which has its own laws and which is a conjecture as to the
conditions of the posthumous existence during which men will un-

dergo further stages of spiritual enlightenment if God has not finished His work with them at the end of their lifetimes. Interpolated into this story is a remarkable passage which has no apparent structural function in the plot as a whole. A Restoration rake and his wife, whom he had ignored in life, are pictured as skeletons who are dependent upon each other, in a ludicrous manner, for aid in holding their joints together. Mr. Raven explains that they are in the process of learning in the afterlife lessons which they failed to learn on earth: "My lord used to regard my lady as a worthless encumbrance, for he was tired of her beauty, and had spent her money; now he needs her to cobble his joints for him! These changes have roots of hope in them . . .: they must at last grow weary of their mutual repugnance, and begin to love one another!" [10]

Mr. Vane is reminded of an earlier and equally curious scene where he watched a costume ball. The dancers are like the rake and his wife in not being fully fleshed; for, although they have bodies, their heads are naked, grinning skulls. In a strikingly powerful passage, as compellingly written as anything by MacDonald's more famous contemporaries, the scene suddenly dissolves:

As if each shape had been but a snow-image, it began to fall to pieces, ruining in the warm wind. In papery flakes the flesh peeled from its bones, dropping like soiled snow from under its garments; these fell fluttering in rags and strips, and the whole white skeleton, emerging from garment and flesh together, stood bare and lank amid the decay that littered the floor. A faint rattling shiver went through the naked company; pair after pair the lamping eyes went out; and the darkness grew round me with the loneliness. For a moment the leaves were still swept fluttering all one way; then the wind ceased, and the owl floated silent through the silent night. [11]

When Mr. Vane remarks upon the similarity of the two scenes, both involving skeletons and flesh, his mentor explains that the lord and lady skeletons are at an earlier stage of their posthumous education since they have no flesh at all, even temporarily: "Those [the dancers] are centuries in advance of these [the lord and lady]. You saw that these could even dress themselves a little! . . . They are pretty steadily growing more capable, and will by and by develop faces; for every grain of truthfulness adds a fiber to the show of their humanity." [12] (I suspect that the title of

C. S. Lewis's retelling of the Cupid and Psyche legend, *Till We Have Faces,* may stem from this passage; for Lewis's indebtedness to MacDonald has been repeatedly emphasized not only in this study but also in Lewis's own works.)

This passage is the last of the embodiments of the spiritual education to which I shall refer. The reader will note that there is something different in this image of the skeleton acquiring flesh as the soul acquires wisdom. It is, for one thing, explained by Mr. Raven, who represents the preaching side of MacDonald himself. We might not, in fact, make the connecton between the symbol and the thing symbolized without such explanation; in the other instances which I have cited, the connection is at least subconsciously apparent, whether or not we know about MacDonald's theory of the spiritual education. This case, for all its imaginative originality, is less universally comprehensible simply because it *is* so original. The eastward journey, the trip to another world, Darwinian evolution, metempsychosis, sexual maturation, and growing up in general—all of these images have something in common with the acquisition of flesh by a skeleton, but resemble such fleshing-out less than they do each other. The difference lies, I think, in that they are ideas which the reader has met before, now placed in a context which imparts to them a new symbolic suggestiveness. We can learn to see the meanings inherent in the most commonplace things of the world, but the *entirely* alien is more difficult to interpret.

IV *Meaning, Technique, and "Talent"*

As I trust I have shown, MacDonald did succeed in finding a number of ways to suggest the same idea. In the process, however, he managed to suggest more than the idea of the spiritual education itself involves. MacDonald's didactic muse commanded him to tell us his message, and he did his best, which was surely good enough. But meanwhile, the symbolic muse was suggesting ways by which larger meaning might be simultaneously loaded into his words and images. For there is something fundamentally human and independent of mere religious doctrine in the mysterous process of growth, education, maturation, and general individual progress. MacDonald's symbolic language manages to communicate something true to those who disbelieve utterly in God and in the afterlife. It is this way with all of the great mythopoeic works of the human imagination: they are morally and psychologically "true," quite aside from and specific doctrine which their authors "intended" them to dramatize. We need not believe in hell, purgatory, and paradise; but Dante is, nevertheless, a profound teacher. We may doubt that there is any literal truth in the Book of Genesis, but we cannot doubt that man is in some sense a fallen creature. I am impressed by MacDonald's theological system, given its premises, as the most reasonable, consistent, and coherent I have ever confronted; but I do not have to *believe* those premises about God's existence, His infinite justice, and His infinite mercy. There is a fundamental human truth behind the symbols through which MacDonald expresses his debatable doctrine of the spiritual education, and I find that fact the most convincing of his literary virtues.

We could, if we chose, multiply instances. The image of the many-chambered house with its subterranean passages and uncharted corridors could, for instance, be catalogued in all of its appearances; and it could be correlated at every point with MacDonald's psychological insights about the nature of the mind. We could also write a book a thousand pages long, but I believe that the point has been sufficiently stressed that MacDonald's peculiar literary gift consisted in his having, so to speak, two muses who worked together most effectively in his symbolic fiction to give it a richness of texture and a universality of truth rare in the history of literature.

For the works of George MacDonald do exist in the context of literary history. After he has been analyzed and after his techniques have been examined, there still remains the problem of trying to assess his significance both as a man of his time and as an artist aspiring to transcend his time and to tell later ages something which they need to know. Since MacDonald's former fame has vanished and since interest in him has only recently begun to be revived by scholars and critics, it may be difficult to make such an assessment, but it must be attempted.

CHAPTER 7

Some Conclusions

I *"A Set of Curious Chances"*

GEORGE MacDONALD'S fiction certainly provides us with a valuable "case history." His literary excellences and faults are traceable to the interaction between a number of conditioning factors, of which I have discussed six: (1) the circumstances of his life, (2) the peculiarities of his private religion, (3) the climate of opinion and taste in his time, (4) the influence of his consciously didactic purpose on his works, (5) the inherent natures of the genres in which he wrote, and (6) the special quality of his imaginaton. It is difficult to subject a writer of the highest rank to this sort of cause-and-effect analysis simply because he transcends many of these conditioning factors in his art. We learn more of the nature of the Elizabethan stage from the study of Kyd and Jonson than from Shakespeare, for Shakespeare cannot be explained in terms of his world; he has to be accepted in terms of his unconditioned genius, though knowledge of his time is helpful. It is clear, however, that MacDonald *was* subject to circumstances, and thus we can examine the way in which each factor affected the nature of his works. To a large extent, we can tell why his conventional novels were bad art but commercially successful and why his limitations as an artist did not hamper his best works.

The circumstances of MacDonald's life were, of course, among the most important of the chances which shaped his work. If he had not found an artistic model for his symbolic fiction in the works if the German Romantics, he might never have written his few masterpieces. If he had not rebelled against the stringent Calvinism of his native Aberdeenshire, he might never have been moved to devise a less harsh counterview of the nature of God's mercy and justice. If he had not felt a vocation to the ministry and subsequently offended his congregation with his "heresies," he certainly would not have decided to be a professional writer—nor would his work have had the conscious didactic purpose which is one of its most important features. Finally, of course, the fact that many of his novels were, at least in part, autobiographical resulted incidentally in his being the founder of a new outburst of Scots regional literature, complete with dialect and "local color." But we do not say that all these "ifs" *doomed* MacDonald to write a certain kind of fiction. Such biographical circumstances could have befallen a person who was not a potential artist.

The nature of MacDonald's private religion is, on the other hand, of unmitigatedly paramount importance. It lent itself ideally to embodiment in symbolic rather than in realistic form; and it was of a nature which, once symbolized, can be reinterpreted almost endlessly. Certainly, if MacDonald had not been almost forced by his reasoning to postulate that the afterlife must involve additional probation and time for the soul for God to do his work of bringing even the reprobate to enlightenment, he would not be so attractive to twentieth-century exponents of Christian orthodoxy such as Chesterton, Fremantle, Lewis, and Auden. All of them are presumably delighted to find a Catholic purgatory in MacDonald's works—and happy to overlook the fact that he insisted that damnation cannot be permanent even for the devil. Perhaps the atheist or humanist cannot swallow the direct expression of MacDonald's ideas in his sermons, but he can discern human truth in their literary, implicit expression.

The fact that MacDonald did, after all, live in the Victorian age likewise conditions his work. His decision to be a professional writer, brought about by his wish to reach a wide audience with his message, demanded that he cater to the tastes of his day. I suspect, for example, that, despite his attempts to justify the near-compulsiveness of the happy endings in his novels, he may at times have felt twinges of both artistic and philosophical conscience about the practice; for it contradicted his theory that, though God's work of saving each soul might not be finished in this world, there are future worlds where it would eventually be accomplished. One notes the lack of total fulfillment in the fantasies, in writing which MacDonald was suiting himself, not popular taste. The Victorian reader's tendency to look for wish fulfillment in the popular novel is probably the reason that so many of MacDonald's heroes, whose virtue in their humble station is

treated as a reproach to their social "betters" of notorious immo-
rality, turn out to be unacknowleged nobility—as is the case in
Malcolm, The Marquis of Lossie, and *Sir Gibbie.* The popular
taste again led MacDonald to undermine his argument that virtue
is its own reward.

Still another aspect of the deleterious effect of conventional
tastes upon MacDonald's novels is his insistence, especially prominent in the later novels, upon setting his stories in genteel English
surroundings rather than among the humble Scots peasantry
whose spirit he could convey so much more compellingly. This is
one of the chief reasons why *Alec Forbes of Howglen* is MacDonald's best novel—its hero goes back to his Aberdeenshire birthplace and becomes a farmer, enriched but not "spoiled" by his
universtity education. *Heather and Snow* is another novel un-
marred by a shift in scene to the English country house where
MacDonald himself was never at home, although his readers liked
to pretend or dream that they were.

As for the influence of Victorian taste (at least of the mass
market for which he wrote) upon MacDonald's imaginative fiction, it was largely repressive; but this fact may have been to advantage in the longer view of literary history. *Phantastes* was a
"failure" because it did not reach the wide readership which he
sought. His attempt to create a hybrid form in *Adela Cathcart,*
with its conventional genteel framework varied by interspersion
of some of MacDonald's finest fantasies for adults, also failed to
sell; and it also failed to convince anybody that literary fantasy
has any therapeutic value. Among MacDonald's symbolic works,
only the stories for children achieved much popularity. Discouraged, he largely abandoned the genres to which his genius was
best suited, and only with *Lilith,* written nearly at the end of his
creative life and published when he was seventy, did MacDonald
try again to write adult fantasy. C. S. Lewis is justified in be-
moaning the fact that MacDonald lived in the wrong age, but
there is another way of looking at it. It is possible that Victorian
prudery and religious conventionality may have caused MacDonald to put his more unconventional ideas into the obscure and
resonant form of symbolism. With the corrosive freedom which
our age has granted to its Henry Millers, MacDonald might have
had his say in the novel only—a form unsuited to his genius.

The effect of MacDonald's deliberate didacticism, unlike those factors which I have just listed, permits us to draw some general conclusions which need not be limited to MacDonald himself, but which provide us with a basis for theorizing about didactic literature as a whole. The "preachy" novel is unlikely to last. Its "message" is, in the course of history, likely to become old-fashioned and merely quaint, especially if it is embodied in the form of direct exposition by the characters rather than dramatized by their experiences. Even in our own century, Aldous Huxley's Peacockian novels and André Gide's direct moralizing are becoming outdated as the ideas which they propound have become sufficiently familiar to be trite when directly expressed. On the other hand, even the stock-in-trade philosophical themes of the dramatic novelist—the novelist who *shows* his reader the interplay of ideas in action rather than simply *telling* him—are never stale because we are free to admire technique even when we can no longer get excited about content. MacDonald was deficient in this sort of dramatizing technique. His characters tend to become mere spokesmen; his plots, mere vehicles. In the realistic novels, his didacticism is rarely exciting.

Furthermore, MacDonald's personal message itself was, as I have suggested, especially inappropriate to dramatization in the novel form. Since the novel deals with credible men and women in a social context, its indigenously appropriate content is social and ethical rather than religious and metaphysical. Even Graham Greene's more successful religious novels involve the *practice* of religion in this world rather than its transcendent features. George MacDonald, with his primary concern for the otherworldly, was simply not sufficiently mundane to write good realistic fiction of a consciously didactic nature.

In the preceding passages, I have also been considering the nature of the fictional genres, even while I was discussing the nature of didacticism. It must, in fact, be emphasized that it is the *interaction* of these conditioning factors which resulted in the excellences and deficiencies of MacDonald's works. It is impossible to discuss didacticism apart from the form it takes. Nevertheless, the inherent qualities of the fictional genres account for certain aspects of MacDonald's work which cannot be otherwise explained —if they can be "explained" at all. If the novel must be lifelike, the fantasy must be dreamlike. The psychoanalysts tell us that the occurrences in our dreams are mythic, their settings are symbolic, and their characters are archetypal; and we find the same events, places, and people in dream fiction. Fantasy is, by its very nature, dramatization of the abstract and general, of the universally human rather than of the peculiarly individual. If there are sexual motifs in Lilith's figurative rape of Mr. Vane or in the Light Princess's symbolic passage through puberty, they refer not to particular people but to universal experiences, in that the war between the sexes finds us all enlisted in one army or the other and the ordeal of sexual maturation happens to everybody.

This study of MacDonald's works shows most clearly, in fact, that the realistic and symbolic fictional modes are inherently opposites. Lifelike versus dreamlike; particular, general; probable, improbable; this world, the other world; real people, spiritual essences; time, eternity; objects, symbols—a whole constellation of opposites seems to develop from a comparison of the realistic and the fantastic genres. Because MacDonald wrote both kinds of fiction—unlike most authors, who stick to one or the other—study of his work provides a challenge to contrast within a single corpus these two opposites.

Finally, there is the conditioning factor of George MacDonald's special type of imagination. No amount of literary sophistication, no degree of familiarity with Swedenborg, Boehme, or Blake, and not even a gift for eloquent expression in words can make a man a genius of symbolic fiction. Didactic purpose is likely to turn into allegory—where every symbol means one thing only—unless, like MacDonald, the writer has that mysterious knack for finding universal, multifarious, evocative symbols in which to embody his ideas. Both C. S. Lewis and W. H. Auden call MacDonald's strange gift a "mythopoeic imagination." No doubt a Jungian like Frye would praise his power to turn fantasy characters into "archetypes," but a Freudian like Prescott would praise MacDonald's "symbolic" power. If these are separate gifts, then MacDonald had them all; but I am inclined to believe that they are likely to appear together in whoever has them. C. S. Lewis has expressed some provocative suggestions about MacDonald's "gift," whatever we call it:

The critical problem with which we are confronted is whether this art—the art of myth-making—is a species of literary art. The objection to so classifying it is that the Myth does not essentially exist is *words* at all. . . . I do not know how to classify such genius. To call it literary genius seems unsatisfactory since it can co-exist with great inferiority in the art of words. . . . It begins to look as if there were an art, or a gift, which criticism has largely ignored.[1]

Although I have tried to define it, the question of what the "mythopoeic imagination" is, the question of why one man has it while another lacks it, is less answerable. Furthermore, MacDonald's indubitable possession of the gift cannot by itself explain the nature of his works; *all* of the "conditioning factors" which I have considered seem to have operated *collectively* to produce one of the remarkable literary careers in history.

II   *"He Must Build Churches Then"*

George MacDonald's permanent "rank" as an artist must remain secondary, for there is no way to excuse his artistic faults—sentimentality, verbosity, preachiness, sheer lack of craft. Even his finest fantasies are too frequently disfigured by the same blights, especially of style, which make his conventional novels generally painful reading today. Yet there are many signs that MacDonald's eclipse will not last. The reviews of the 1954 *Visionary Novels* edition were generally favorable. The praise of such renowned men as Auden and Lewis cannot be ignored, and it seems likely to precipitate a renewal of critical interest in MacDonald's fantasies. The publication of Robert Lee Wolff's study, despite its flaws, is likely to arouse more interest than a less sensational work could. It seems at least probable that MacDonald will be given more attention in future literary histories. He is a more important writer, I venture to say, than a number of his better-known Victorian contemporaries—Arthur Clough, Charles Kingsley, Walter Pater, perhaps even William Morris. These men are important in and with reference to their time, but they say little to later generations; MacDonald's minor fame survives, however, because he speaks to a time later than his own. In his imaginative fiction, his limited doctrinal "message" achieves a universality, because of its suggestive expression in symbolism, which transcends time—though in his novels, being more explicit in their preachiness, are already rather stale. He has built churches: they will last to be used (and admired if not used) by whatever posterity may notice them. Meanwhile, whether or not the scholarly and critical communities carry further the gradual reappraisal of MacDonald which they have begun, he will be read and enjoyed. Perhaps his time is not yet, despite the signs to the contrary; but even so he is likely to be "rediscovered" now and then, to the benefit and delight of people who love to read.

Notes and References

Many of the references below are to passages from MacDonald's novels, which involve a rather frustrating bibliographical problem. While it is customary to cite volume- and page-numbers from first editions, these are now extremely rare; no complete collection exists in the United States, although that at the Houghton Library of Harvard University is nearly complete. Later one-volume "popular" editions (the first editions are usually in three volumes) are available everywhere, however, so that anyone who wished to check the references below would not have to go to Harvard to do so. The pagination, of course, is not the same as in the first editions; therefore I have cited *both* volume and page numbers from first editions and, parenthetically, chapter numbers. MacDonald's chapters, fortunately, are quite short, so that quoted passages can be found easily, even when first editions are not available.

In a few cases, MacDonald revised his work or issued essentially similar but slightly changed collections (notably of essays and short stories) at different times and under different titles. Such instances are noted below; I have usually cited the most complete collections rather than the earliest, especially since the latter often were in relatively scarce periodicals.

For the sake of condensation, I have given at their first appearance abbreviated titles of works frequently cited, and mentioned them by the short titles thereafter. I have also grouped together into a single note multiple references when they occur in the same paragraph of the text, citing them in the order of their appearance.

Chapter One

1. G. K. Chesterton's obituary article appears in the London *Daily News*, September 23, 1905, p. 6.
2. New York, 1954; hereafter cited as *Visionary Novels*.
3. New York, 1947; hereafter cited as *Anthology*.
4. Robert Lee Wolff, *The Golden Key: A Study of the Fiction of George MacDonald* (New Haven, 1961); hereafter cited as *Golden Key*.

5. *Anthology,* 11.

6. *Golden Key,* 389.

7. Greville MacDonald, *George MacDonald and His Wife* (New York, 1924), p. 72; hereafter, following the practice of Robert Lee Wolff, I cite this work as *GMDW.*

8. *The Portent* (London, 1864), 82–83 (Ch. VII).

9. *Anthology,* pp. 12–13.

10. The translation of the Spiritual Songs is now an extremely rare book. When J. M. Bullock wrote his useful "Bibliography of George MacDonald," *Aberdeen University Library Bulletin,* Vol. 30 (February, 1925), he reported that only one copy was known. Recently another copy has turned up; a slight revision dated 1873, it is now in the Houghton Library of Harvard University. Both appear to have been printed privately and circulated only among MacDonald's friends.

11. Greville MacDonald also discusses the Ruskin-La Touche entanglement in his *Reminiscences of a Specialist* (London, 1932), and it has been most recently and authoritatively studied in *The Letters of John Ruskin to Lord and Lady Mount-Temple* (Columbus, 1964), ed. and with an introduction by John L. Bradley. Both Greville Mac-Donald and Professor Bradley base their examinations of George Mac-Donald's relationship with Ruskin upon the Ruskin Collection of the Yale University Library.

12. See Sir William Duguid Geddes, "George MacDonald as a Poet," *Blackwood's Magazine,* cxlix (March, 1891), 361–70. J. M. Bullock, in his "Bibliography of George MacDonald," states that "there is reason to believe that Sir William wrote this article with a view to the selection of MacDonald as Poet Laureate." I do not know what reason Bullock had in mind, but two bases for his conjecture seem plausible: MacDonald was a Scot like Geddes, and the Laureateship was then vacant since Tennyson had just died.

13. C. S. Lewis, *The Allegory of Love* (London, 1936), 232.

Chapter Two

1. The word "orts" means table-leftovers and vaguely suggests garbage, which is why I call this title "unfortunate." Like some other MacDonald collections, *A Dish of Orts* (London, 1893) was published under other titles and with slightly different contents, as noted in the Selected Bibliography. The 1893 volume was not the earliest version, but it is the most complete, and I have therefore cited this volume here and hereafter. I have not given it the shortened title *Orts* because that is the title of an earlier and less complete collection. Because the essays are short, it should be relatively easy to find citations in editions other than the 1893 version which I cite.

2. Miss Mary MacDonald, Greville MacDonald's adopted daughter, informed me in a private letter of 1958 that the library was, to the best of her knowledge, broken up when George MacDonald died in 1905.

3. *Weighed and Wanting* (London, 1882, 3 vols.), I, 47 (Ch. III).

4. References are to *Unspoken Sermons, Third Series* (London, 1889), 229; *Unspoken Sermons, Second Series* (London, 1885), 113; and *The Miracles of Our Lord* (London, 1870), 42. References hereafter are to *Sermons I* (London, 1867), *Sermons II*, and *Sermons III;* and to *Miracles*.

5. *Robert Falconer* (London, 1868, 3 vols.), II, 129 (Ch. XXXVI); *Phantastes* (London, 1858), 323 (Ch. XXIV); *Miracles*, 43; *Sermons II*, 204–5.

6. *Sermons III*, 155; *Sermons I*, 81.

7. *Sermons III*, 126–27.

8. *Adela Cathcart* (London, 1864, 3 vols.), I, 271–72 (Ch. VI).

9. *Robert Falconer*, I, 157 (Ch. VI).

10. *Miracles*, 243–44.

11. *Sermons II*, 49–50.

12. *A Dish of Orts*, 246; *Miracles*, 153; *Sermons III*, 251; *A Dish of Orts*, 258.

13. Swedenborg's *Heaven and Its Wonders and Hell* (trans. J. C. Ager, New York, 1956), 53; Boehme's *Contemplations* (from the collection entitled *Personal Christianity*, New York, n.d.), 175; Law's "An Appeal to All Who Doubt," from *The Liberal and Mystical Writings of W. Law*, ed. W. Scott Palmer (London, 1908). Boehme was the earliest of these three Renaissance mystics, writing in the early 1600's and probably influencing Law and Swedenborg, both of whom wrote in the early 1700's. All three references are taken from Evelyn Underhill's *Mysticism*, Meridian edition (New York, 1955), 263; Miss Underhill's study was originally published in 1911.

14. *Sermons I*, 100–101.

15. Evelyn Underhill, *Mysticism*, 167 ff.

16. *Wilfrid Cumbermede* (London, 1872, 3 vols.), Ch. LIX (I have not been able to consult a first edition of this work).

17. *Sartor Resartus*, Book Second, Ch. IX (I have not seen a first edition); *Mary Marston* (London, 1881, 3 vols.), I, 194–95 (Ch. XI); and MacDonald's introduction to an English translation of the German Novel *For the Right*, by Karl Emil Franzos, trans. Julie Sutter (London, 1888), vii.

18. *Donal Grant* (London, 1883, 3 vols.), Ch. XXIX (I have not been able to see a first edition).

19. *A Dish of Orts*, 24–25.

20. *At the Back of the North Wind* (London, 1871), Ch. VIII. (I have not seen a first edition.) Hereafter, this work is cited as *North Wind. A Dish of Orts,* 33.

21. *Paul Faber, Surgeon* (London, 1879, 3 vols.), III, 78 (Ch. XLVIII).

22. *Wilfrid Cumbermede,* Ch. XLVIII; *What's Mine's Mine* (London, 1886, 3 vols.), I, 60 (Ch. V); *Adela Cathcart,* II, 169–70 (Ch. XI).

23. *A Dish of Orts,* 46.

24. From "George MacDonald: A Personal Memoir," by Ronald MacDonald, in *From a Northern Window* (London, 1911), 66–67. Ronald MacDonald's contribution to this collection of essays by various authors appears on pages 55–113 of the volume.

25. *Donal Grant,* Ch. V; *Weighed and Wanting,* I, 26 (Ch. II).

26. *Wilfrid Cumbermede,* Ch. LV; *Annals of a Quiet Neighborhood* (London, 1867, 3 vols.), Ch. VII.

27. *Wilfrid Cumbermede,* Ch. LV.

28. *The Portent,* iii; *A Dish of Orts,* 317; *A Dish of Orts,* 93.

29. *A Dish of Orts,* 314–15.

30. The Coleridge tradition regarding Fancy and Imagination, which contributes something obscure but useful about the distinction between the two, stems from *Biographia Literaria* (1817). It was carried on less perceptively by Leigh Hunt's *Imagination and Fancy* (New York, 1845) and John Ruskin's *Modern Painters,* III, ii, Ch. III, 7 (London, 1856). MacDonald apparently follows Ruskin.

31. *A Dish of Orts,* 25; *A Dish of Orts,* 316–17.

32. *Lilith* (London, 1895), 61; *Phantastes,* 131–32.

Chapter Three

1. *Wilfrid Cumbermede,* Ch. LXV.

2. Wolff points out the difference between the original version of *The Portent,* published serially in *The Cornhill Magazine* (May, June, July, 1860), and the later revision published as a volume in 1864. See *Golden Key,* 397 and n.

3. *Golden Key,* 306–14.

4. Margaret Dalziel, *Popular Fiction 100 Years Ago* (London, 1957), 99–100.

5. *The Marquis of Lossie* (London, 1877, 3 vols.), Ch. XLIII.

6. Greville MacDonald, *GMDW,* 26.

7. See Patricia Thomson's *The Victorian Heroine* (London, 1956), 24–36.

8. Greville MacDonald, *Reminiscences of a Specialist,* 100.

9. *Anthology,* 18.

10. *Anthology,* 12.

11. *Castle Warlock* (London, 1880, 3 vols.), I, 1–2 (Ch. I). Later "popular" editions of this work were entitled *Warlock O'Glenwarlock.*

Chapter Four

1. *Golden Key,* 118.
2. *Adela Cathcart,* I, 222 (Ch. V).
3. *Golden Key,* 118.
4. *Visionary Novels,* vi.
5. "The Golden Key" was first published in *Dealings with the Fairies* (London, 1867), hereafter cited as *Dealings.*
6. *Visionary Novels,* vi.
7. See Chesterton's introduction to *GMDW,* 11.
8. Herodotus describes the Hyperboreans in Book IV, 32–36. Wolff traces MacDonald's reference to the same idea to a verse by James Hogg (see *Golden Key,* 151 and 399n.), but he does not tell us where Dante—another source mentioned by MacDonald—deals with it; I, too, have failed to locate the reference.
9. *At the Back of the North Wind* (London, 1871), 363–64 (Ch. XXXVI).
10. *Anthology,* 17.
11. *GMDW,* 318.
12. *Phantastes,* 9–11 (Ch. II).
13. *Phantastes,* 320 (Ch. XXV).
14. *Phantastes,* 271–72 (Ch. XXI).
15. *GMDW,* 548–49.
16. *Lilith,* with an introduction and a paraphrase of the earlier version by Greville MacDonald (Centennial Edition, London, 1925), xviii–xix.
17. For an account of the traditional Lilith story, see Angelo S. Rappaport, *The Folklore of the Jews* (London, 1937), 96–97. Rappaport cites as his source "the book of Pseudo-Sirach (Sepher Ben Sira), ed. Steinschneider, 1858," and it may have been this version from which MacDonald got the story. See also Joshua Trachtenberg, *Jewish Magic and Superstition* (New York, 1939), 36–37 and 277–278. Lilith is also mentioned in the Walpurgisnacht section of Goethe's *Faust.* There is a poem about her by Dante Gabriel Rossetti, and a novel called *Lilith* by Mrs. E. D. N. Southworth (London, 1881). Just recently the motif has appeared again, in another novel called *Lilith* (New York, 1961), by J. R. Salamanca, and in a science-fiction novel called *The Light of Lilith* (New York, 1961), whose author is given as "G. McDonald Wallis"—possibly a pseudonym and perhaps not a coincidence, though no influence is detectable. For some reason, George MacDonald was fond of the name "Lilith." There is a horse

with that name in *St. George and St. Michael* (London, 1876, 3 vols.), a woman in "The Cruel Painter."

18. *Lilith*, 278–81 (Ch. XXXIX).

19. *Lilith*, 303 (Ch. XL).

20. *A Dish of Orts*, 314–16.

21. *Visionary Novels*, vii.

22. *At the Back of the North Wind*, 123–24 (Ch. XI).

23. *Phantastes*, 193 (Ch. XIV).

Chapter Five

1. *Lilith* (1925 Centennial Edition), 369.

2. *Lilith* (1925 Centennial Edition), xv, n. Greville MacDonald apparently errs in supposing that Boehme originated the idea of a correspondence between the so-called four elements and the four temperaments or "humours." The elements may be traced to Empedocles (490–430 B.C.); the "humours" to Hippocrates (ca. 460–377 B.C.); and the correspondence between them is the idea of the medical followers of Hippocrates. Greville MacDonald also appears to be mistaken in stating the correspondence between air and the sanguine and between fire and the choleric; for the ancients and their medieval successors had it the other way around. See Charles Singer, *A Short History of Medicine* (New York, 1928), 33–35.

3. *Lilith*, 23 (Ch. IV).

4. F. C. Prescott, *The Poetic Mind* (Ithaca, 1959), 222–23. This edition is a reprint of the now rare original edition of 1922.

5. *The Poetic Mind*, 106.

6. *The Poetic Mind*, 106–7.

7. This passage from Shelley's *Defence of Poetry* is cited in Prescott's *The Poetic Mind*, 111.

8. *The Poetic Mind*, 113.

9. Northrop Frye, *Anatomy of Criticism* (Princeton, 1957), 304.

10. C. G. Jung, *Two Essays on Analytical Psychology*, trans. R. F. C. Hull (New York, 1956), 106. Originally published in Switzerland as *Über die Psychologie des Unbewussten* (1943) and *Die Beziehung zwischen dem Ich und dem Unbewussten* (1945).

11. C. G. Jung, *Psyche and Symbol*, trans. R. F. C. Hull and Cary Barnes (New York, 1958), 7. This volume consists of a number of Jung's essays assembled by the Bollingen Foundation; the passage cited is from "Aion," Part II, Vol. 9 of *The Collected Works of C. G. Jung* (New York, 1958).

12. *Psyche and Symbol*, 11.

13. *Lilith*, 183–84 (Ch. XXVI).

14. I quote from a personal letter to me from Mr. Lewis, of 1956.

Chapter Six

1. Evelyn Underhill, *Mysticism*, 128.
2. *Dealings*, 308.
3. *Phantastes*, 12 (Ch. III).
4. *Lilith*, 59 (Ch. IX).
5. *GMDW*, 555.
6. See S. Foster Damon, *William Blake: his Philosophy and Symbols* (New York, 1924), 433.
7. *Visionary Novels*, vi.
8. *Dealings*, 302.
9. *Visionary Novels*, i.
10. *Lilith*, 127 (Ch. XVII).
11. *Lilith*, 119 (Ch. XVI).
12. *Lilith*, 127–28 (Ch. XVII).
13. *Anthology*, 14–16.

Selected Bibliography

PRIMARY SOURCES

The following list of George MacDonald's works is based upon the exhaustive "Bibliography of George MacDonald," by J. M. Bullock, as published in the *Aberdeen University Library Bulletin*, 30 (February, 1925). I have largely omitted MacDonald's poetry and translations, both because they are of lesser importance than the works listed and because both exist in an immense variety of entries, both as magazine-published originals and in later collections which frequently involve revisions, and which vary in content. Because the text of my study treats MacDonald's works under certain categories, I have preserved these distinctions in classifying this list.

1. Novels

Adela Cathcart. London: Hurst and Blackett, 1864. 3 vols. It should be noted that this volume contains a number of interpolated short stories which were later published in various collections, but first appeared in *Adela Cathcart*.

Alec Forbes of Howglen. London: Hurst and Blackett, 1865. 3 vols.

Annals of a Quiet Neighborhood. London: Hurst and Blackett, 1867. 3 vols.

Castle Warlock. London: Sampson Low, 1882. 3 vols. This novel was sometimes entitled *Warlock O'Glenwarlock* in later editions.

David Elginbrod. London: Hurst and Blackett, 1863. 3 vols.

Donal Grant. London: Kegan Paul, 1883. 3 vols.

The Elect Lady. London: Kegan Paul, 1888.

The Flight of the Shadow. London: Kegan Paul, 1891.

Guild Court. London: Hurst and Blackett, 1868. 3 vols.

Gutta Percha Willie: or, the Working Genius. London: Henry S. King, 1873.

Heather and Snow. London: Chatto and Windus, 1893. 2 vols.

Home Again. London: Kegan Paul, 1887.

Malcolm. London: Henry S. King, 1875. 3 vols.

The Marquis of Lossie. London: Hurst and Blackett, 1877. 3 vols.

Mary Marston. London: Sampson Low, 1881. 3 vols.

Paul Faber, Surgeon. London: Hurst and Blackett, 1879. 3 vols.
Ranald Bannerman's Boyhood. London: Strahan, 1871.
Robert Falconer. London: Hurst and Blackett, 1868. 3 vols.
A Rough Shaking. London: Blackie and Sons, 1890.
Saint George and Saint Michael. London: Henry S. King, 1876. 3 vols.
Salted with Fire. London: Hurst and Blackett, 1897.
The Seaboard Parish. London: Tinsley Bros., 1868. 3 vols.
Sir Gibbie. London: Hurst and Blackett, 1879. 3 vols.
There and Back. London: Kegan Paul, 1891. 3 vols.
Thomas Wingfold, Curate. London: Hurst and Blackett, 1876. 3 vols.
The Vicar's Daughter. London: Tinsley Bros., 1872. 3 vols.
Weighed and Wanting. London: Sampson Low, 1882. 3 vols.
What's Mine's Mine. London: Kegan Paul, 1886. 3 vols.
Wilfrid Cumbermede. London: Hurst and Blackett, 1872. 3 vols.

2. Short Stories

The Gifts of the Christ Child. London: Sampson Low, 1882. These
    stories had been earlier published in various magazines. Essen-
    tially the same collection was sometimes later republished under
    the title *Stephen Archer and Other Tales.*

3. Full-length Fantasies for Children

At the Back of the North Wind. London: Strahan, 1871.
A Double Story. First printed under this title in *Good Things,* a chil-
    dren's magazine edited by MacDonald, December, 1874, through
    July, 1875, *passim.* First published in book form as *The Wise
    Woman* (London: Strahan, 1875). Published later under both of
    these titles, and also as *Princess Rosamund* and *The Lost Princess.*
The Princess and Curdie. London: Chatto and Windus, 1883.
The Princess and the Goblin. London: Strahan, 1872.

4. Short Fantasies for Children

Dealings with the Fairies. London: Strahan, 1867. This edition con-
    tains most of the shorter fantasies for children, many of which had
    previously been interpolated into *Adela Cathcart* in 1864 (see
    under "Novels" above) or in magazines. Bullock lists several
    stories which were not anthologized. Other and later collections
    incorporating roughly the same material, sometimes together with
    longer works or poems, are entitled *The Light Princess and Other
    Fairy Tales, Works of Fancy and Imagination,* and *Fairy Tales of
    George MacDonald.* Most such titles have appeared in more than
    one edition; I have used the title of the earliest such anthology.
    Two of the stories in this collection, "The Light Princess" and

"The Golden Key," are long enough to have been published separately from time to time.

5. Full-length Fantasies for Adults

Lilith. London: Chatto and Windus, 1895. Of the many reissues of this work, the most important is the Centennial Edition (London: George Allen and Unwin, 1924), which contains an introduction and a paraphrase of the earlier version, both by Greville Mac-Donald.

Phantastes: A Faerie Romance for Men and Women. London: Smith, Elder, 1858.

6. Short Fantasies for Adults

The Portent and Other Stories. London: Smith, Elder, 1924. This is the only collection which treats the shorter fantasies for adults as a separate genre. Many are also included in *Works of Fancy and Imagination* (London: Chatto and Windus, 1871; 10 vols.) and interpolated into *Adela Cathcart* (see under "Novels" above) in 1864. Only *The Portent* has been issued as a separate volume (London: Smith, Elder, 1864). That story was first written as a shorter tale in *Cornhill Magazine*, May-June-July, 1860, *passim*.

7. Essays, Sermons, Criticism, and Other Prose Nonfiction

A Dish of Orts. London: Sampson Low, 1893. This collection of essays was first published as *Orts* (London: Sampson Low, 1882), which did not contain the important essay entitled "The Fantastic Imagination." That essay originally appeared as the introduction to a collection entitled *The Light Princess and Other Fairy Tales* in 1893. Later editions of essentially the same collection of essays were later sometimes entitled *The Imagination and Other Essays*. I have cited *A Dish of Orts* because it is the earliest edition containing *all* of MacDonald's important essays. It does not, however, contain several minor essays, for which the reader is referred to Bullock.

The Hope of the Gospel. London: Ward, Lock, Bowden, 1892. Sermons.

The Miracles of Our Lord. London: Strahan, 1870. Sermons.

The Tragedie of Hamlet, Prince of Denmarke. London: Longmans, Green, 1885. A critical edition of Shakespeare's First Folio text, with many comments by MacDonald.

Unspoken Sermons. London: Strahan, 1867.

Unspoken Sermons, Second Series. London: Longmans, Green, 1885.

Unspoken Sermons, Third Series. London: Longmans, Green, 1889.

SECONDARY SOURCES

The following list is selective in that it omits a number of brief and not especially helpful magazine essays and reviews, but it includes all of the critically important works about MacDonald.

AUDEN, W. H. Introduction, *Visionary Novels of George MacDonald*, ed. Anne Fremantle. New York: Noonday Press, 1954. In this brief, informal piece Auden contributes some valuable ideas toward the understanding of MacDonald's *Lilith* and *Phantastes*.

CARTER, LIN. "Beyond the Gates of Dream." This is a preface to an edition of *Phantastes* (New York: Ballantine Books, 1970), part of Ballantine's "Adult Fantasy" series. Carter's remarks are not of great value and contain a few minor errors, but the reissue has been valuable to the revival of interest in MacDonald.

JOHNSON, JOSEPH. *George MacDonald: A Biographical and Critical Appreciation*. London: Pitman, 1906. Rushed into print immediately after George MacDonald's death, this is a largely worthless work, deficient in understanding and full of factual errors; but it accurately reflects the adulation which MacDonald received from his contemporaries.

LEWIS, C. S. Introduction to *George MacDonald: An Anthology* (New York: Macmillan, 1947), which is a collection of moral and religious maxims culled from MacDonald's works by Lewis. The MacDonald selections are not especially important, but the introduction by the volume's compiler is brilliant and perceptive; it has probably done more toward reviving interest in MacDonald than any other study.

MACDONALD, GREVILLE. *George MacDonald and His Wife*. Introduction by G. K. Chesterton. New York: Dial Press, 1924. This massive volume contains all that is known about MacDonald's life, besides a good deal of rather inexpert critical commentary.

WOLFF, ROBERT LEE. *The Golden Key: A Study of the Fiction of George MacDonald*. New Haven: Yale University Press, 1961. An important, largely Freudian study, it is characterized by stimulating and penetrating psychological interpretations but by uneven and sometimes unreliable literary criticism. Wolff approaches MacDonald's works as symptomatic of their author's neuroses, and he manifestly dislikes MacDonald. Wolff's study also contains a careful and thorough tracing of influences upon MacDonald's work, especially by the German Romantics, in whom he finds many parallels.

Index

(Under George MacDonald's name are listed references to significant events in his life, to his works, to his most important ideas, to his typical symbols and myths, and to his plots, characters, and settings.)

Alger, Horatio, 28
Anderson, George K., 10
Auden, W. H., 18–19, 79, 81, 89, 96, 104, 131, 134, 139, 142, 143
Austen, Jane, 31, 114, 121
Austin, Alfred, 26

Baedeker, Carl, 80
Barrie, J. M., 72
Blake, William, 32, 102, 112, 142; *Jerusalem*, 130–31
Bloom, Edward A., 10
Boehme, Jacob, 33, 38, 108–9, 130, 142
Borrow, George, 114
Bradner, Leicester, 10
Brontë, Emily, 119; *Wuthering Heights*, 114
Browning, Robert, 112
Bullock, J. M.: "Bibliography of George MacDonald," 146 *n.* 10 and 12, 153
Bulwer-Lytton, E. G., 17
Bunyan, John: *Pilgrim's Progress*, 102
Burns, Robert, 72; Burnsian, 57–58
Byron, George Gordon, Lord, 23
Byron, Lady, 24

Calvinism, 33, 138; Calvinist, 20
Carlyle, Thomas, 17, 41
Carroll, Lewis, *see* Charles Dodgson
Carter, Lin, 87

Chaucer, Geoffrey, 22, 53–54
Chesterton, G. K., 18, 81, 139
Christ, Jesus, 85, 109, 130
Clemens, Samuel, 18; *Huckleberry Finn*, 105; *The Prince and the Pauper*, 84
Clough, Arthur, 143
Coleridge, Samuel Taylor, 49
Collins, Wilkie, 17, 58
Cowper, William, 30
Cruse, Amy: *The Victorians and Their Reading*, 17

Dalziel, Margaret: *Popular Fiction 100 Years Ago*, 65
Damon, S. Foster, 9, 130–31
Dante Alighieri, 27, 119, 137; Dantean, 19; *Divine Comedy*, 102
Darwin, Charles, 132; Darwinian, 136
Defoe, Daniel, 114
Dickens, Charles, 17, 20, 25, 45, 48, 58, 70, 74, 113, 119; *Bleak House*, 68; *Hard Times*, 61; *Oliver Twist*, 64
Dodgson, Charles, 17; *Alice in Wonderland*, 26, 81; *Through the Looking Glass*, 95
Dostoevsky, Feodor, 31

Eliot, T. S.: *The Waste Land*, 76, 123

Faulkner, William, 53–54

Fiedler, Leslie A.: *No! in Thunder,* 129
Fielding, Henry, 114
Fletcher, Phineas: *The Purple Island,* 87
Fremantle, Anne, 19, 139
Freud, Sigmund, 21, 41–44, 82; Freudian, 19, 41–45, 78, 81, 119, 131, 142; post-Freudian, 123
Froude, J. A., 17
Frye, Northrop, 142; *Anatomy of Criticism,* 114–15, 119, 121

Gide, André, 141
Gielgud, Sir John, 27
Gilbert and Sullivan: *Ruddigore,* 68
Gilder, Richard Watson, 18
Good Words for the Young, 75–76, 77
Greene, Graham, 141

Herbert, George, 22
Herodotus, 83
Hill, Octavia, 46, 68
Hoffmann, E. T. A., 87
Holmes, Oliver Wendell, 18
Hunt, Leigh, 49
Huxley, Aldous, 141

James, Henry, 31, 114
Jonson, Ben, 138
Jung, Carl Gustav, 116–21; Jungian, 142

Kafka, Franz, 87, 112, 122
Kapstein, I. J., 10
Keats, John: "La Belle Dame Sans Merci," 92; "Ode to a Nightingale," 128
Kierkegaard, Søren, 102
Kingsley, Charles, 18, 24, 143; *Water Babies,* 83, 84
Kyd, Thomas, 138

La Touche, Rose, 25, 69
Leibnitz, Baron Gottfried Wilhelm von, 35, 83

Lewis, C. S., 30, 74, 87, 121, 139, 140, 142–43; *George MacDonald: An Anthology,* 19–22 passim., 31, 71, 85; *The Great Divorce,* 19; *Surprised by Joy,* 18–19; *Till We Have Faces,* 136
Longfellow, Henry Wadsworth, 18

Macaulay, T. B., 17
MacDonald, Alec (brother), 23, 68, 90
MacDonald, George, Sr. (father), 20–23, 68, 87
MacDonald, George:
  a) life: birth, 20; at public school in Aberdeen, 21; at University of Aberdeen, 21, 23; cataloguing a library "in the far north," 21–22; graduated from Highbury College, London, 23; tubercular attack, 23, 90; at first parish in Arundel, Sussex, 23–24; marriage, 24; resigned from parish, 24; acquired residence at Bordighera on Italian Riviera, 25
  b) ideas: coincidence in realistic fiction, 48; dreams as source of religious truth, 43, 88–89, 103–104; fancy and imagination, supposed distinction between, 49; fantasy in literature (includes remarks by both MacDonald and the author, under "fantasy" and such synonymous terms as "symbolism," "mythopoeia," "visionary literature," "imaginative literature," etc.), 28–31, 48–49, 60–61, 75 ff., 88 ff., 142–43; happy ending, theory and practice in the novel, 47, 55–57, 61, 64, 106; mystic personality (in others and in MacDonald himself), 38–41, 43; nature, symbolic meaning in, 38; prenatal memory, 43; sexuality, 44–45, 69, 76–78, 92, 118, 123; time, God's limitation

in (when dealing with human beings), 34, 107

c) archetypes, symbols and myths: buildings, castles and many-chambered houses (as symbols of the mind's compartmentalization), 41–42, 73, 81, 85, 104; cellars, caves, and underground labyrinths (as symbols of the lower levels of the psyche), 73, 82, 104; death (as symbol of entering a new life), 83–84, 102, 110; education, spiritual (as myth dramatizing spiritual enlightenment as a process), 125 ff.; evolution as myth dramatizing spiritual enlightenment), 132–33; journeys (especially toward the East, as myth dramatizing "the mystic way" of spiritual enlightenment), 40, 122, 128; metempsychosis (as myth dramatizing a step in spiritual enlightenment), 80, 133; Shadow (as archetype representing the "dark half" of the personality), 92–93, 99, 116–117; the Waste Land (as symbol of immaturity and sexual sterility), 76–78, 96, 101, 105, 134; also, plot as myth, 120–122, and characters in fantasy as archetypes, 115

d) typical characters in novels: stereotypes, 52, 66–67; admirable artisans (cobblers, bookbinders, carpenters, blacksmiths, etc.), 45, 70; handicapped saints and children, 70–71, 82; "stickit minister," 64, 69–71

e) didacticism, 27, 30, 46–47, 125 ff., 140–41

f) style: in prose, 53–55, 86–87; in verse, 26

g) Works:
Adela Cathcart, 36, 43, 60–61, 77, 85, 86, 140
Alec Forbes of Howglen, 21, 52, 61–64, 66–67, 74, 140

Annals of a Quiet Neighborhood, 40, 47–48, 56–57, 66
At the Back of the North Wind, 28, 43, 71, 82–84, 86, 95, 104, 121, 127–28
"Carasoyn, The," 80
"Castle, The," 85–86
Castle Warlock, 73
"Cruel Painter, The," 85
David Elginbrod, 25, 57, 58, 60–61, 66, 85
Dealing with the Fairies, 76
Dish of Orts, A, 32, 38, 42, 44, 49, 50
Donal Grant, 41–42, 47, 58, 73
Double Story, A, 28, 84–85
"Fantastic Imagination, The," 103
"Far Above Rubies," 26
"Giant's Heart, The," 81
"Golden Key, The," 28–29, 78–80, 81, 86–87, 103, 105, 121, 127–28, 132–34
"Grey Wolf, The," 85, 119
Guild Court, 70, 82
Gutta Percha Willie, 28
Hamlet (critical edition of), 26–27
Heather and Snow, 60, 67, 70, 73, 140
"History of Photogen and Nycteris, The," 80
Hope of the Gospel, The, 32
"Light Princess, The," 28, 76–80, 81, 86–87, 88, 101, 103, 105, 119, 123, 129, 134, 142
Lilith, 18, 29, 50–51, 86–87, 94–102, 104–10 passim., 112, 117–23 passim., 127–32 passim., 134–36, 140, 142
Lost Princess, The, see A Double Story
Malcolm, 57–58, 65, 67, 70, 71, 119, 140
Marquis of Lossie, The, 58, 65–66, 70–73 passim., 119, 140
Mary Marston, 41, 67
Miracles of Our Lord, The, 32, 34, 37

Paul Faber, Surgeon, 43, 57, 59, 132

Phantastes, 18–19, 25, 29, 34, 50–51, 77, 86–94, 104–5, 107, 117, 121, 127, 128–29, 131, 140

Poetical Works of George Mac-Donald, The, 26

Portent, The, 22, 29, 49, 59, 85, 86, 111

Princess and Curdie, The, 19, 28, 82, 86, 119, 132

Princess and the Goblin, The, 19, 28, 81–82, 85, 86, 88, 119, 127, 132

Princess Rosamund, see A Double Story

Rampolli: growths from a long-planted root, 27

Robert Falconer, 34, 36–37, 66–67, 68

Rough Shaking, A, 60

St. George and St. Michael, 28

Sartor Resartus, 41

Sir Gibbie, 53–54, 57–58, 60, 70, 82, 140

"Sketch of Individual Development, A," 39–40, 43, 82

Thomas Wingfold, Curate, 60, 66

Twelve Spiritual Songs of Novalis (trans.), 24

Unspoken Sermons, 32, 34–35, 39; *Second Series,* 32, 34, 38; *Third Series,* 32, 34–36, 38

Vicar's Daughter, The, 68

Visionary Novels of George MacDonald (ed. by Anne Fremantle), 18, 143

Weighed and Wanting, 33, 47

What's Mine's Mine, 43

Wilfrid Cumbermede, 40, 43, 47–48, 56–57, 58, 68–69, 106, 123

Wise Woman, The, see A Double Story

Within and Without, 23–24

MacDonald, Greville (son): *George MacDonald and His Wife,* 18, 19–22, 25, 31, 68, 69, 86, 94, 108–9

MacDonald, Helen, née MacKay (mother), 21, 43, 88

MacDonald, Isabella, née Robertson (grandmother), 68

MacDonald, John (brother), 23, 90

MacDonald, Louisa Powell (wife), 18, 20, 23–24, 119

MacDonald, Ronald (son), 46–47

Malory, Sir Thomas: *Morte Darthur,* 90

March, William: *The Bad Seed,* 130

Marcus, Steven: *The Other Victorians,* 77

Maurice, F. D., 18, 32

Melville, Herman, 114, 119–20

Miller, Henry, 140

Milton, John, 102

Morris, William, 45, 70, 143; *The Wood Beyond the World,* 87

Nabokov, Vladimir: *Lolita,* 129–30

Novalis, 24, 27, 87

Osborne, Charles, 69

Pater, Walter, 143

Peacock, Thomas Love, 114; Peacockian, 141

Peake, Mervyn, 87

Philbrick, Charles H., 9

Platonic, 107, 114

Poe, Edgar Allan, 85, 119

Pope, Alexander, 35

Prescott, Frederick Clarke, 142; *The Poetic Mind,* 111, 113–15

Radcliffe, Anne, 59

Reade, Charles, 58

Richter, Jean Paul Friedrich, 87

Ruskin, John, 17, 25, 45, 49, 69, 70

Schlegel, A. W., 111

Scott, Sir Walter, 72; *Rob Roy,* 70

Shakespeare, William, 55, 112, 138; *Othello,* 115

Shaw, George Bernard, 30, 31

Shelley, Percy Bysshe, 26, 112, 113

Sidney, Sir Philip: *Defence of Poesie,* 70
Snow White and the Seven Dwarfs, 119
Spenser, Edmund, 87; *The Faerie Queene,* 90
Stowe, Harriet Beecher, 18
Swedenborg, Emmanuel, 33, 38, 130, 142

Tennyson, Alfred, 18, 26
Thackeray, William Makepeace, 17, 55, 112; *Vanity Fair,* 64
Tolkien, J. R. R., 87
Trollope, Anthony, 17, 119
Twain, Mark, *see* Samuel Clemens

Underhill, Evelyn: *Mysticism,* 38–40, 122, 127

Victoria, Queen, 25
Virgil, 19
Voltaire, Francois Marie Arouet de: *Candide,* 35, 83

Wolff, Robert Lee: *The Golden Key: A Study of the Fiction of George MacDonald,* 19–20, 21, 22, 29, 41, 45, 59, 64, 69, 76, 78, 87, 88, 90, 92, 102, 111, 120, 133, 143
Wordsworth William, 44, 49, 129; "Immortality Ode," 77

DATE DUE

GAYLORD			PRINTED IN U.S.A.